EXTRA INNINGS

PRAISE FOR MAX SCHUMACHER AND EXTRA INNINGS

"Max Schumacher has given his working life to baseball, particularly the Indianapolis Indians. His management skills helped advance the careers of a host of major leaguers and Hall of Famers. This book tells the stories behind Max's huge contributions to baseball."

—Carl Erskine, Dodgers pitcher, 1948 – 1959

"After fifty years in baseball, I've learned that the true heart and soul of the game can be found in the thousands of people who make Minor League Baseball a labor of love. That's what Max Schumacher's book is all about. He is the epitome of what makes Minor League Baseball special. It all started with that 'sack of peanuts' as a youngster in the 1940s. Reading *Extra Innings* by Max makes me cherish every story, just like he cherished each and every peanut in that sack!"

—George Grande, Cincinnati Reds TV broadcaster

"This is a very deserving story of a baseball lifer. Max Schumacher is directly responsible for the great success of baseball in Indianapolis. We've been connected for thirty-seven years, and I'm proud to call him a friend. He will always be a friend of the game."

—Clint Hurdle, Pittsburgh Pirates manager

"We won four consecutive American Association championships in Indianapolis with Max from 1986 to 1989 en route to developing the 1994 Championship Montreal Expos, and along the way he taught me to view every baseball as a five-dollar bill. Like Branch Rickey before him, Max Schumacher, hands down, is far and away the best professional baseball club operator of his generation. He did the right thing for coaches, players, the league, the parent club, the National Association, and fans; its in the book!"

—Dan Duquette, former Montreal Expos, Boston Red Sox,
and Baltimore Orioles manager

"Max Schumacher has accomplished some incredible things in his lifetime, and it makes for interesting reading. He has associated with and influenced so many, including myself. I totally enjoyed my managing experience with the Indianapolis Indians and feel the time spent there was the springboard to fulfilling one of my lifelong dreams of managing at the MLB level."

—Cecil Cooper, Five-time Boston Red Sox and Milwaukee
Brewers All-Star, former Houston Astros manager

"Max was a dignified individual who ran a first-class operation from top to bottom. Also, he loved baseball and understood the nuances of the game.

—Dave Dombrowski, Boston Red Sox President of Baseball
Operations

EXTRA INNINGS

MY LIFE IN BASEBALL

by Max Schumacher with Mark Montieth

INDIANAPOLIS, INDIANA

Published by Blue River Press
Indianapolis, Indiana
www.brpressbooks.com

Distributed by Cardinal Publishers Group
A Tom Doherty Company, Inc.
www.cardinalpub.com

ISBN: 978-1-68157-146-1

Cover Design: John Ilang-ilang
Book Design: Rick Korab, Korab Company Design
Cover Photo: AP Images
Interior Photos: Courtesy of the Indianapolis Indians unless otherwise noted
Editor: Dani McCormick

Printed in the United States of America

10 9 8 7 6 5 4 3 2 1   19 20 21 22 23 24 25 26 27 28

DEDICATION

I dedicate this book to my darling wife, Judy. Thank you for your partnership and commitment to our marriage and the raising of our four wonderful children, now responsible and successful adults. Your love and support helped me to fully enjoy the mostly good times and successfully navigate the tough times.

— *Max*

To my parents, Margaret and Richard Montieth, who got me into the game and kept me from straying into foul territory.

— *Mark*

TABLE OF CONTENTS

FOREWORD

I met Max Schumacher in the fall of 1946 when we entered Shortridge High School together as wide-eyed freshmen. It didn't take long for us to connect, and our bond has remained strong in all the years since.

I was a run-of-the-mill member of the freshman football team, and Max was the student manager. Early on, he got my name wrong when we lined up to receive equipment, confusing "Lugar" with "Lauter," but we got to know one another well before long. I eventually had to give up football because of allergies, and from that point limited my participation in sports to golf and track while Max played baseball.

We both worked on the *Echo,* Shortridge's daily student newspaper, and were together often away from school. We spent many hours in one another's homes and various activities. I conducted a table tennis tournament at my house over Christmas break that Max won one year, defeating me for the championship. I played an offensive style and Max played defensive. Just as in all areas of his life, he was steady and didn't make mistakes. I also hosted a croquet tournament in the summer. Max won that, too, beating me out at the last stake.

We attended a lot of Indianapolis Indians baseball games together as well— first with our fathers, and then on our own when I became old enough to drive. Those summer afternoons and evenings were an important part of our childhoods and remain a happy memory for me. Aside from the enjoyment of watching the games, they afforded us time to talk about a lot of things that were important to teenage boys in the early 1950s.

We were never out of touch for long after going away to college—Max to Butler University and I to Denison University. We communicated constantly and were ushers in each other's wedding. After becoming Mayor of Indianapolis in 1968, I worked with Max and others to arrange the sale of Victory Field from the Perry family's estate to the city. It was important to me, because I was fully aware of the impact the Indians had on the city as both an entertainment option and economic force.

That impact has been severely underrated over the years, as have Max's contributions. People might be more familiar with the Pacers and Colts, but a professional baseball franchise has been operating in Indianapolis for more than 130 years, and they play 70 home games each season. The Indianapolis Indians provide exciting, pleasant, low-cost entertainment in the spring and summer months. Since moving to their downtown stadium in 1996, they have become an essential part of the city's landscape.

Nobody has been more important to the Indians' success than Max, and nobody has been a more long-lasting and faithful friend to me. Here's one example:

While in high school, I organized the Indianapolis Young Republican Club. Max was the secretary-treasurer. We performed flunky jobs that nobody else wanted to do to help the party's efforts in the city. Max was so responsible with the funds we collected that he searched high and low for the best interest rate and wound up depositing them in a bank in suburban St. Louis. Years later, when I made my first run for Mayor in 1967, he withdrew the money and donated it to my campaign. By then the club members had grown and scattered, and it was time to shut down the organization. It only amounted to a few hundred dollars, but that deed says a lot about Max's integrity and business acumen.

Former US Senator Richard Lugar and Max Schumacher transferred home plate from Bush Stadium to the new Victory Field.

I was back in Indianapolis in October of 2018 for a ceremony dedicating the redeveloped plaza that had been named in my honor on the south side of the Indianapolis City-County Building. As I looked out toward the audience, one of the first people I saw was Max. Like me, he's 86 years old. He's had some health concerns in recent years, and it wasn't easy for him to get there, and it certainly wasn't comfortable for him to be sitting there on that chilly day. That tells you all you need to know about Max's loyalty and friendship.

Max's tremendous personal qualities were evident throughout his years with the Indians as well, and Indianapolis is much better as a result. I'm so happy that he's finally getting the opportunity to share some of his memories, and I hope people gain a better understanding of all he's done for the Indians and for Indianapolis.

—Richard Lugar, Former US Senator and Mayor of Indianapolis

PREFACE

Like a lot of kids, I was introduced to baseball by my father.

He made his living as a musician, but he was a huge fan of baseball—so big, in fact, that if the Indianapolis Symphony Orchestra had a concert during the World Series, he would take a radio on stage with him and flip it on between songs to catch the score of the game.

He wasn't a great athlete, but he loved to hit fungo balls to me. He was left-handed and didn't even use his right arm when swinging the bat. That always amazed me. He'd swing the bat like a tennis racket and connect with balls all day long. He would stand in an alley near our house and I'd run over to an open area by the railroad tracks. He'd hit one really, really high and shout "Five dollars!" Meaning he would give me $5 if I caught it. I always did, but he never paid off. I didn't expect him to, because it was just for fun.

He introduced me to the Indianapolis Indians in the 1940s, and would take me to several games each summer. He let me out of the car on 16th Street to get in line for tickets while he parked the car across the street in the old CYO Field. I'd start walking toward the ticket window, then break into a jog, and then start running as fast as I could. There was just something about a baseball game that drew me in. The ballpark was like a magnet to me.

The Indians had some great teams in the late '40s when future Hall of Famer Al Lopez was the manager, and my dad and I attended a lot of games together. After my dad caught up with me and we got inside the gate, he headed straight for the concession stand to buy a sack of peanuts. First thing, every time. Those kind of memories never leave you. Little did I know that one day I would be working in that stadium.

I was hired by the Indians in January of 1957 as the ticket manager, and became the general manager in 1961. I've been with the franchise ever since, through championship seasons and losing seasons, through a procession of players, managers, and major-league affiliates, and through the move from our antiquated stadium on West 16th Street to our beautiful downtown ballpark.

During all those years, I've never had a reserved parking space. I just parked wherever I could in the employee lot. And, yes, I often jogged to the front door. The lure of the ballpark never left me; besides, I had a desk job and needed all the exercise I could get.

I always enjoyed going to work and facing the challenges of the day. Early in my time with the franchise, we occasionally were fighting for mere survival. All I knew to do was go to work every day and try to maximize income and minimize expenses. If I had been a business major at Butler University instead of a journalism major, I might have thought the challenges were too great. Sometimes, I guess, it's good to be naïve.

Although I wound up working for the Indians for more than 60 years, I might have left after only a few years if a planned opportunity had come through.

One day in the late '50s, I got a call from the band director at Butler University, who was a friend of my father's. The university was looking to hire an athletic publicity director, and he wanted to know if I would be interested.

I was. I did not enjoy working for our general manager Ray Johnston and was newly married, so the chance to improve my income was inviting. Butler officials were talking about adding $1 to the price of football and basketball season ticket prices, which they expected to raise $7,000 to be used for the salary of the newly added position. That was considerably more than I was earning with the Indians at the time, and an offer I would have to take seriously.

The band director later called me back, however, and told me he had good news and bad news. The good news was that Butler officials had decided to raise the ticket prices. The bad news was that the money wasn't going to be used for an athletic publicity director.

I had firm offers for other jobs in baseball in later years, but none of them felt right for me after I became established with the Indians.

I became acquainted with Buzzie Bavasi, the longtime general manager of the Los Angeles Dodgers, during my last year in the Army in 1956. I met him through my sister, Joan, who was a secretary for a man named Bill McCormick, who had gone to DePauw University with Bavasi. Through Mr. McCormick I wrote letters to Bavasi to inquire about a job. He sent back a polite rejection each time.

Later, though, Buzzie offered a potential opportunity. Danny Kaye, the comedian and actor, was part of a group that bought Seattle's new franchise in 1976. He was friends with Buzzie and turned to him for help to get it started. Buzzie told me I probably could get on Kaye's staff as an assistant of some kind in the front office. I wasn't interested because I liked my situation with the Indians and liked living in Indianapolis. As I remember, I turned it down immediately on the telephone without talking it over with anyone or even thinking about it for long.

Through Buzzie, I got to know Peter, his son. Peter was hired to help a group from Indianapolis land a major-league franchise in the '80s. They attended the winter meetings one year with a model of the city's new stadium, the Hoosier Dome. It had been built for football, but they were claiming it could be made suitable for baseball as well. The model they took to the meetings, however, was set up as a football stadium.

I became acquainted with Peter during those meetings, and he later became the founding president of the Toronto Blue Jays. He called one day to ask if I would come to Toronto as his assistant. I didn't know exactly what that would have entailed. I might have talked about it briefly with Judy, but it still came down to the fact I loved what I was doing with the Indians and living in Indianapolis. I called Peter back a couple of days later and told him I wanted to stay in Indianapolis.

I also had a chance to go to work for the National Association of Professional Baseball Leagues in St. Petersburg, Florida, which is the governing body of all minor-league baseball teams. Hank Peters was working there and I had gotten to know him well. He offered me a position as Vice President, but that job didn't provide a rooting interest for me. I liked the idea of really caring about the team you're working for. There's nothing like being in a pennant race, when every game is important and you experience the thrill of victory and the agony of defeat. And there's no greater feeling than winning a championship and knowing you had a part in it.

I just didn't have the kind of ambition that drives one to work in the major leagues. It never appealed to me, really, even amid the financially challenging times for the Indians—or for my family. I never had the feeling that I had to make a lot of money to be successful or that we needed to live extravagantly. Judy and I didn't have to have the biggest house or the nicest cars. I remember our board chairman Hank Warren once congratulating me for finally unloading an old car I had been driving and buying a "decent" one.

Looking back, I don't regret turning down any of the opportunities that came my way. I never grew tired of going to the games, and will always be proud of the positive impact the Indians have had on the city. I take pride in helping provide wholesome, low-cost entertainment for the masses, and it's rewarding to hear fans say it's the best bargain in sports.

As a native of Indianapolis and graduate of an Indianapolis high school, Shortridge, I also enjoy how our new ballpark helped change the face of downtown. Many fans who were against moving from the park we had called home since 1931 have since told me how much they appreciate the modern facility, and the fact ticket and concession prices remain reasonable. The new park, in turn, has greatly enhanced our financial stability. Survival is no longer an issue.

I suffered a stroke on July 3, 2016, and retired in November of 2017. I don't get around as well as I'd like, but I still serve as Chairman Emeritus. The greatest asset any business executive can leave his or her successor is a stable, well-run organization, and I believe I was able to do that.

I still attend games as often as I can. I don't run through the parking lot anymore, but I'm still excited to go. I just hope the kids attending our games today feel the same emotional pull from the ballpark that I did. And I hope the readers of this book enjoy the memories I've accumulated throughout my years with the Indianapolis Indians.

—Max Schumacher

PLAYING BALL

I was fortunate that the area where I grew up in Indianapolis didn't have a Little League baseball program. That might sound strange coming from a kid who loved baseball, but the kids in my neighborhood were forced to show initiative. They weren't well-organized and we had no uniforms, but we learned how to arrange games and get along with one another without adult supervision.

We began by playing on our grade school playground at 46th Street and Central Avenue, on a diamond built for softball. It was a small field, naturally. The way the diamond was laid out, a righthanded hitter would hit the side of the school building behind left field if he really connected with one. Anyone who's ever played baseball can tell you, when you hit one just right, it's a great feeling. Breaking a window on the school building numbed that feeling a bit, but it was still kind of fun. We weren't trying to break windows, but it made for a dramatic moment when we did.

Fortunately, we never got in trouble for it. This was in the mid-1940s, during World War II, and school administrators liked the fact boys were playing ball instead of roaming the streets and finding ways to cause trouble. Some people might consider breaking school windows to be trouble, but nobody complained about it or made us pay for the damages. Whenever it happened, one of us would manage to get into the school and retrieve the ball so we could start playing again.

Still, the nuisance of breaking a window and having to retrieve the ball, and probably our guilty consciences as well, finally motivated us to build our own diamond. Some of the kids in my neighborhood and I, 15 to 20 in all, got together and constructed one on a vacant lot on the southwest corner of 46th Street and College Avenue. We cut down the weeds and bushes and constructed something resembling a baseball diamond. We didn't have a dirt infield, a pitcher's mound, or fences, but it was passable. And we usually were able to round up enough kids to play games, with nine per side.

We put on our own World Series and played a best-of-seven set of games. We might have had umpires occasionally, but when we didn't, the catcher would call balls and strikes. It was an honor system. We had occasional disagreements, but worked them out ourselves.

It was the opposite of how boys play baseball today. Now kids play in highly-structured games on manicured diamonds in fancy uniforms with coaches directing their every move and their parents watching—and often

yelling—from the bleachers. There's nothing wrong with that, I guess, and kids probably improve more in that environment. But I doubt they have more fun than we did. We learned a lot from playing on our own, and not just about baseball. We learned initiative and how to govern ourselves in a pressure-free atmosphere.

Caddy-corner from our diamond, on the northeast corner, sat Chaplin's Drug Store. None of the kids liked

Young Max sits with (left to right) his sister Joan, mother Virginia, and sister Dorothy on the front steps of their home on North Winthrop.

Mr. Chaplin because he griped at us all the time when we went into the store. Some of the kids even stole from him as a way of getting revenge. They'd pick up a *Saturday Evening Post,* stuff several comic books inside and then pay for only the *Post.* It was much easier to steal from someone who treated us poorly all the time. I didn't, but I was aware it was going on and ignored it.

One day, during one of our "World Series" games, he walked out of his store and tossed a ball across the street to us. It was a rare display of generosity, totally out of character. I've often thought if he had given us a ball two or three years earlier he would have been much better off. We would have been customers instead of thieves. It was a business lesson that would serve me well later in life. You need to treat the customers well and maintain good public relations.

I finally got a chance to play organized baseball when I was 11 or 12 years old and became eligible to play in the Junior League program. My first team was called the Leopards. A lot of teams had animals for their nicknames back then—Lions and Tigers and Bears, that kind of thing—but I wanted a unique name. I didn't know of any other teams called Leopards, so we went with that.

Our uniforms consisted of blue jeans and a plain white T-shirt, with no numbers or lettering. Most of the teams in the league had really nice uniforms, so we were determined to get uniforms of our own the following year. We got together to visit businesses on the north side of town and solicit donations. You might get $3 or $4 from the dry cleaner, $4 or $5 from the pharmacist, a few dollars from the barber, and so on. I don't recall if we asked Mr. Chaplin for money; probably not, since none of the kids would have wanted to go in and talk with him.

Once we got sponsorship, we called our team the North Side Merchants. The businesses didn't receive any recognition for their donations, they just did it as a favor to the kids. A man on the North Side made the uniforms for us. We all went up there together to get them, and he showed us how to "blouse" our socks by taking the top of the stocking and rolling it down a little from the top. That's how the kids liked to do it then, just like the pros.

It was a great feeling to have uniforms like the other teams—it made you feel like a real ballplayer. Ours had the letters "NSM" on the front. We had no numbers or names, but at least we looked like a real team.

We were pretty good, too. We did well in the regular season, but we had a bad experience in our playoff game when the father of one of the boys on the other team kept yelling insults at one of our players.

Dick Falender, one of our outfielders, was a one of our group of neighborhood friends who played sports together throughout the year. He was Jewish. Most of us were Protestants, but we didn't even think about someone's religion. This man sat in the stands and had his mouth going all day long, shouting "Jew-boy" this and "Jew-boy" that. Nobody tried to stop him, but it seemed to affect Dick. It's amazing now to think someone could get away with that without other adults intervening. Dick later was a high school teammate of mine, and went on to become a successful dentist.

I attended Shortridge High School, one of the finest high schools in the country at the time. It didn't have a freshman baseball team then, but I played my sophomore, junior, and senior years. I was a backup second baseman as a sophomore and then a starter my final two years. I was elected captain as a senior. I played basketball as a freshman, but was the last player cut from the team as a sophomore and junior, so baseball was my only sport my final three years. I was the student manager for the football team all four years, however.

My baseball coach was Jerry Steiner, who also coached basketball. He had played both sports at Butler University and played professional basketball for the Indianapolis Kautskys. Fortunately for me, he restarted the baseball program at Shortridge after it had been dormant for several years.

He was a great guy, but he had a fiery temper. We rode to away games in cars, and sometimes I rode with him. Even if we won the game he'd be really angry if we had played badly. He had a car with a manual transmission, and if he was upset about the game he wouldn't bother to engage the clutch when shifting — he'd just grind the gears. It was like it helped him blow off steam. It made for a rough ride home, that's for sure.

I hit just one home run in my high school career, so it was memorable. Our home field was Diamond Number 6 at Riverside Park. It didn't have a fence, and there was a softball diamond beyond deep left field.

I was normally a singles hitter. I'd try to get a base hit or a walk, or even let the ball hit me in the back. I just wanted to get on base any way I could and let somebody else move me around. More than anything, I loved to score runs. But one day when we were playing Broad Ripple High School, I really got into one. The ball sailed over the leftfielder's head, and with no fence to stop it, it rolled onto the next diamond, still in play. I guess that means it was an inside-the-park home run, technically—with "park" being the city park, not the baseball diamond.

I'd like to say I glided across home plate into the waiting arms of my celebrating teammates, but it didn't work out that way. I had to slide to beat the throw, and landed on my bat. Ward Walker was the next batter and he hadn't picked it up. He was a three-sport athlete, but baseball probably was his weakest of the three and he didn't understand the nuances of the game. Believe me, it hurts when you slide and land on your bat. Ward greeted me by slapping me on the back and yelling, "That-a-baby, Maxie!" I didn't feel like celebrating at the moment, though, and yelled, "I don't need to hear all that, just get the damn bat out of the way!" It kind of took the edge off my moment of glory.

I later had an RBI single amid a three-run rally in the sixth inning that gave us an 8 – 7 victory, and we snapped Broad Ripple's 24-game win streak, so I went home happy.

I was a decent hitter—.319 my junior year and .323 as a senior—and a solid defensive second baseman, so I wanted to keep playing after high school. Toward the end of my senior year, Coach Steiner took me out to meet the baseball coach at Butler to see if some scholarship aid might be available. I had little choice but to go there for college because my family couldn't afford to pay for housing on a campus. By attending Butler I could live at home and drive back and forth to classes. A little scholarship money would have been really helpful, though.

Butler's baseball coach was the legendary Tony Hinkle. He was best known for coaching basketball, and later would be inducted into the Naismith Basketball Hall of Fame, but he also coached football and baseball and served as athletic director.

That's right, he coached three sports and was the athletic director as well. If that wasn't enough to keep one man busy, he was the groundskeeper for the baseball diamond, too. He wore a swim suit when he mowed the grass, raked the dirt, packed the mound, and put down the foul lines. By the end of the season, he'd be almost as black as an African American from being out in the sun so much.

The day Coach Steiner took me out to meet him, we found him in the training room. He was wearing a cast on his leg because he had caught his foot in the mower while cutting grass. Coach Steiner said he believed I was good enough to compete on the college level and asked if it would be possible for me to receive some scholarship money. Coach Hinkle just said, "Well, kiddo, we have a fine program here and Butler's a great school, so after you enroll we'll make an announcement about the start of practice. Then you can come out for ball and away we go."

In other words, no scholarship for ol' Max. I was going to have to make the team as a walk-on. I quickly realized why, too. Mr. Hinkle already had a lot of players who were better than I. Some of them played three sports and only took up a partial scholarship from the baseball program.

I didn't make the varsity team as a freshman, so I just intended to watch the games from the bleachers. I wound up getting a lot more than I bargained for, though. When I showed up to watch the first game, Charlie McElfresh, the equipment manager, said, "Kiddo, I found a uniform for you." It didn't match those of the varsity players, but I was pleased to have it. I settled in at the end of the team bench to watch the upperclassmen play, but when Butler's turn to bat came in the bottom of the first inning, Mr. Hinkle leaned over from the other end of the bench and said, "Hey, Schuey, coach third base!"

I continued doing that throughout my freshman and sophomore

seasons. That's normally the head coach's job, but Mr. Hinkle liked to watch the game from the bench. He did just about everything from there. If he needed to change pitchers, he would just shout out to a player and wave him in and call out to the pitcher being removed and motion him to the bench.

He gave baserunning signals from there, too, and in a unique way. To signal for a player to steal a base, he'd lift the front cover of the scorebook sitting on his lap. The problem was, he'd been doing that for so long most of the other teams knew the signals, too. When it became obvious other teams were pitching out and throwing out our runners at second base, he called us together and said, "From now on, the signal doesn't count if I don't have my legs crossed." So that was the variation — book flap up and legs crossed meant a steal, for the rest of that game at least.

He didn't bother with signals for bunts. You might be nearly to home plate and he'd call out, "Push them along!" It seemed obvious he was tipping off the opposition, so finally my senior year I got up enough nerve to ask, "Mr. Hinkle, don't you think that if you're yelling that out to me while I'm standing near home plate, the catcher can hear it, too?"

"Do you think he believes me?" he said, smiling.

That was just his sense of humor, though. Mr. Hinkle was a really good coach, all things considered. He had the ability to develop players, sometimes even taking athletes from other sports and turning them into good baseball players. One example was Keith Greve, a star on the basketball team who was from a small high school, Waveland, that didn't have a baseball team. Mr. Hinkle convinced him to come out for baseball and made him into a productive pitcher. He once threw a six-hitter to beat Purdue.

Mr. Hinkle was an amazing guy, and was fun to play for. He'd pitch batting practice, and we had a lively infield practice, too. He didn't have a temper, and he knew what he was doing at all times. I even have fond memories of the bus rides to away games. Most of the guys fell asleep by the time we left the university parking lot, but I could never sleep on the bus. I'd move up front and sit near Mr. Hinkle and a few other teammates and play word games.

The highlight of my mostly mediocre playing career came in May of my senior season, in a game against DePauw in Greencastle. I was perfect from the plate, hitting four line-drive singles, all of which landed in virtually the same spot about 20 feet behind second base in center field. Mr. Hinkle, who, remember, rarely stood up during games even to change pitchers, was so excited for me that he jumped to his feet and applauded enthusiastically.

We won the game 6 – 1, but my thunder was stolen by our pitcher Norm Ellenberger, who threw a no-hitter. Ellenberger, who went on to become a longtime college basketball coach, also hit a grand slam and drove in all but one of our runs.

Naturally, his name was in the headlines in the Indianapolis newspapers, and he was featured in the articles about the game as well. My greatest claim to fame as a player was nowhere to be found, overshadowed by one of the all-time best performances by a Butler player.

Our teams at Butler weren't great—we were around .500 most of the time—but I had such a great experience playing college baseball that I wanted to continue playing after graduating from Butler in June of 1954.

I knew I was going to be drafted into the military because at that time all males had a two-year obligation to join one of the branches. I was hoping to be drafted as soon as I graduated, but I had to wait six months. During that time, I worked for the Indianapolis Parks Department as a member of the staff for Junior League baseball. I helped run the office and went out into the community to help give clinics for the younger kids, who reminded me of myself when I got started playing in a white T-shirt. We offered instruction and I umpired games, too.

I finally was drafted into the Army in early December of 1954 and was sent to Fort Leonard Wood in Missouri for basic training. I then was transferred to Fort Sheridan in Illinois, north of Chicago.

I had a great experience in the Army, too. I played in the post's intramural basketball league and on the baseball team that competed against semipro teams in the Chicago area. It was high-caliber baseball, but the post later disbanded the baseball team and formed a fast-pitch softball team instead. I had never played competitive softball, but I wanted to keep playing "ball," as Mr. Hinkle would say, and that was the only way to do it.

We competed against the other post teams on the Fort Sheridan grounds. My team didn't win the league championship, but the winning team was entitled to pick up two players from all the other teams in the league and continue playing. I was chosen from my team.

The primary purpose of the "all-star team" was to compete in the Fifth Army tournament in Fort Carson, Colorado. As part of that preparation, we played other teams in the Chicago area. The highlight of that experience was the time we went to Aurora to play a team featuring a pitcher named Harvey Sterkel. He was in the early stages of a career in which he would win 91 percent of his games while pitching 30 no-hitters and 15 perfect games. He's now a member of the Amateur Softball Association Hall of Fame, and he remains a legendary figure in the sport.

Harvey's goal was to pitch a perfect game every time he played. When we faced him, he struck out every batter the first time through the lineup. When I went to bat the second time, I was determined to at least put the ball in play. I stood in the front of the batter's box, choked up on the bat and hit the ball hard off Sterkel's glove. It ricocheted to the second baseman, who threw me out at first base for the third out.

When I went out to second base to play defense, the fans were standing and cheering. I asked the base umpire, "What's with the standing ovation?"

"Oh, that's because you moved the ball," he said. "You hit a fair ball."

"So what?"

"This guy's idea of a perfect game is to strike out every batter, and you put the ball into play."

Imagine that. I got a standing ovation for a groundout, one to four to three.

We later traveled to Fort Carson by train for the tournament. We were eliminated early, and that was essentially the end of my athletic career. It was time to join the real world. ●

In 1957, fresh out of the Army, Max was thrilled to begin his career as the Indianapolis Indians' ticket manager.

LEARNING TO WORK

I never considered myself poor growing up, but my family wasn't affluent by any means. While I wasn't made to go out and find a job to help support the family, I constantly was looking for ways to earn money. That became a guiding force in my life and served me well as an adult. My father made a living as a musician, which wasn't an easy thing to do. He was a charter member of the Indianapolis Symphony Orchestra, for which he played bassoon and contrabassoon. He also led his own band, the Indianapolis Concert Band, which played at a variety of places around Indianapolis, including the Indianapolis Motor Speedway. And he gave saxophone and clarinet lessons in our home.

My mother didn't take a job until after she and my father divorced, when I was in the seventh or eighth grade. They had been separated several times, and when they finally divorced, my two sisters and I lived with Mother in our home on the near north side, at 44th and Winthrop, while my father moved in with his sister.

Mother took a job in housewares for the L. S. Ayres department store after the divorce, and later worked for a bank. She was a great manager of her modest income, able to stretch a dollar a long, long way. She once told me that, on many days during the Depression, she fed our family of five on one dollar per day. She had no choice but to be a smart money manager because Dad was not. That was one of the conflicts in their marriage.

My first job working for someone else remains my least favorite. As a young boy, I picked raspberries in a small field a short walk from my house one summer. I had to get up early and spend an entire day fighting heat, humidity, and insects. My dad stopped by one day to help me. After that I'd find myself looking over at the outline of my house on the horizon and saying to myself, *I hope Dad will come over.*

I had to take six to eight cartons in a picnic basket and fill all of them with raspberries. After turning in the basket, I received a token, which I could exchange for coins. We all were paid a quarter for each filled picnic basket, so I earned about 50 cents per day.

It was difficult, tedious work, but it taught me a valuable lesson: always have respect for the people who perform menial tasks to earn an honest living.

I became a paper boy when I was about 12 years old. My first route was for the *Indianapolis Times*, an afternoon paper that was part of a national chain. It was regarded as the liberal newspaper in the city, which provided an important balance to the conservative viewpoints expressed by the locally-owned *Indianapolis Star* and *Indianapolis News*.

The *Times* had the smallest circulation and was always struggling to survive. I only had 12 – 15 customers for that route and had to ride my bike over a long distance to reach them all. I graduated from that to the home edition of the evening *News*, with a route in my neighborhood. I earned a much greater profit from that.

I had purchased the route temporarily from a neighbor boy who wasn't able to deliver it for a while. We agreed he would pay me 40 cents for each customer I added while he was away, and I would pay him 40 cents for each customer I lost. I was able to grow the route by five to ten customers by approaching neighbors I knew, who spread the word that I was reliable.

He didn't pay me, however. It was another lesson learned; I should have made him put it in writing.

I then graduated to the *Indianapolis Star,* the morning paper with the largest circulation. I had a dense five-block area on the east side of College Avenue that included about 40 homes. It was a decent-sized route through the week, but practically everyone in that area wanted the paper on Sunday.

I made quite a racket on that route. When I delivered the *Times,* I just threw the papers into the basket on my bike and rode by the subscribers' homes. With the *News,* I put them in a canvas bag that I hung around my neck and started walking. But with the *Star,* I had to use a wagon.

I would pick up the papers at the sub station on Sunday morning at about six a.m. A supervisor would count out the papers on my route and I'd load them into the red wagon. I had built up the sides of the wagon with boards so it would hold all of them. When I began walking, the wagon made an irritating squeaking sound because of all the extra weight. I kept thinking someone would yell at me to hold it down, but it never happened. I was probably like a rooster crowing for the residents of that neighborhood, letting everyone know it was time to get up.

I had this route during World War II. Sometimes I would get a call from the newspaper office and be told a special edition was being published because of some big news related to the war. I would pick up the papers at the sub station and ride my bike up and down the street and shout out the headline of that day. Some people would come out on their front porch and tell me to stop so they could buy one.

Those special editions cost two or three cents per copy. The person buying one would usually give me a nickel and tell me to keep the change. The headlines were nearly always positive, so people were in a good mood and feeling more generous as a result. That was a big deal in my mind—getting a couple of extra cents per sale.

Delivering the newspapers was difficult enough, but sometimes collecting money from the subscribers was worse. Anyone who has ever delivered newspapers has stories of customers who kept putting them off, saying they were busy or didn't have enough change with them at the moment, or perhaps only had a $20 bill. I never carried enough money to make that kind of change. Still, I made about $5 a week from the *Times* route, $10 from the News route, and $15 or $20 from the *Star* route after I paid the district manager what I owed him for the newspapers.

I also worked for two drug stores as a boy. The first was Fisher's Pharmacy at 49th and College. I made 35 cents per hour working at the soda fountain as a grade-school kid. I'd work the same hours as the owner/pharmacist, so some days I worked four hours and some days I'd work ten hours.

I started my second drug store job when I was 15 years old, working for a man named Acky Cardarelli at 30th and College. Jack Benny built his comedy career on pretending to be cheap, but this guy put Benny to shame in real life. I didn't find it amusing, though.

I was hired to work the soda fountain there for 50 cents an hour, but the job wound up entailing a lot more than that. I did everything. Whenever I had a spare minute I had to take bottles off shelves, dust them and put them back, or haul cases of empty beer bottles to the basement. I worked the cash register, too.

Mr. Cardarelli often would leave the drug store and go to lunch, leaving me in charge at the cash register at the front of the store. One time, I was waiting on three very proper-looking older ladies when a blind man came in, tapping his cane and working his way up to the counter. When he finally got there he said, loudly and clearly, "Give me a dozen rubbers." I was a teenager, but I knew what he was talking about. I had sold them many times at the store. This time, however, I was embarrassed because the older ladies were standing there. They took it with a straight face, though.

After I turned 16 and received my driver's license, I began providing delivery service for Mr. Cardarelli. If he had somebody who wanted liquor on a Sunday, he'd give it to me in a sack, tell me how much money to collect for it and send me off in his car—breaking two laws. It was illegal to sell liquor on Sunday in Indiana, and I wasn't old enough to be selling alcohol, much less delivering it to peoples' homes.

After I had been working there for about a year, I began a running dialogue with Mr. Cardarelli that lasted about six months. I was asking for a raise of a nickel per hour. I just wanted to get 55 cents an hour and feel like I was making progress. We would talk about it, but he kept saying no. One time he said, "Do you realize you're asking for a ten percent raise?" And I said, "Yes, but I also know I'm only asking for an additional nickel an hour!"

One day I pushed a little harder and we became a little heated in our disagreement. The next day when I arrived at work, he called me over and said, "I've decided to discontinue your shifts." How's that for telling someone they're fired? It was beautiful.

I said, "Why didn't you tell me that yesterday? I had to ride the bus down here." He said he would give me a dime for the bus. I told him the bus fare was 15 cents. He said he'd give me 15 cents. I said I had to ride it two ways. So he gave me 30 cents and whatever pay I had coming and I was gone.

My shift had been discontinued.

I could have gotten Mr. Cardarelli into a lot of trouble for letting a 16-year-old kid deliver alcohol on Sundays. I could have brought my father into it, and we could have gone to the authorities and reported his violations. But it was a different world then, and I never gave it a thought.

I learned another great lesson, though, one I've passed on to a lot of young people over the years: The boss is always the boss. If you don't like him, leave. He might be a lot of things, but he's always the boss, and there's nothing you can do about it.

I also worked at the State Fair. My dad knew the ticket manager for the fair's special events, such as the races on the dirt track in front of the main grandstand. His name was Stu Parsons, and he was an odd duck. A chain smoker, he was constantly swiping ashes from his shirt.

When you opened his desk drawer, it was filled with ashes.

He liked and trusted me, though, and I had a great experience working for him. I learned how to handle tickets and money, skills that would come in handy in later years, and I learned more about people, too.

My first summer working the State Fair, before my freshman year of college, I was paid 75 cents an hour as a runner. I would go to a ticket-seller in a booth and he would say, "I need 100 $1.80 tickets for horse racing tomorrow," and give me $180. Then I'd go to the next seller and he'd need 100 $2.40 tickets for the show on the main stage, and he would give me $240.

After collecting all the money, I'd walk to the race track's ticket office to get the tickets to deliver to the sellers. When I arrived, the manager would ask, "Is it all there, kid?" I'd say yes, and he'd tell me to put the money in the filing cabinet. He then gave me the tickets to take back to the sellers. Each week, I took the cash collected from all those sellers to the Administration Building, about a quarter-mile away. It's difficult to believe now that a teenager was sent walking among all sorts of people with $10,000 in his possession, but that's what I did.

That summer, we came up about $1,000 short in the ticket office. It was no wonder, with so many tickets being sold for so many events and so much money being handled. It was go-go-go all the time, so it was a ripe setting for stealing money.

I was rehired again the following year, but this time the manager told me he wanted me to sleep in the ticket office to prevent thefts. He gave me a shotgun to put in the corner and told me he didn't want anybody coming into the office overnight. At that point in my life, I had never shot a gun, so I don't know what I would have done if somebody had come through that door at midnight. I slept on a cot. After waking up early each morning, I passed out tickets and change to the ticket-sellers to get them started, then went home to have breakfast and get cleaned up.

I did catch one thief. He was a ticket-seller in the center booth at the race track, the one that drew the most customers. He was a character out of central casting, a heavy-set man who was a car salesman when the fair wasn't in session. He chewed a cigar, but never smoked it. His strategy was to chat up customers while chomping on that cigar and try to distract them from their transaction.

A lot of ticket prices that year ended in 20 cents or 40 cents. Say, for example, someone purchased three tickets at $2.40, for a total of $7.20. If he was given a ten dollar bill, he'd return $2.20 instead of $2.80 and keep the difference of 60 cents for himself. He never deliberately miscounted bills, just the change, because people didn't pay as much attention to that.

I eventually caught on to him, and he knew it. I didn't confront him, but he somehow knew that I knew, so he gave me $20 folded up in a tiny envelope to buy my silence. He didn't say it in so many words, but he was hoping I wouldn't report him to the boss. I took the envelope to the ticket office and put it on the top shelf, then told the boss what had happened.

The boss said, "Kid, just keep it. We're going to fire him anyway, so to hell with him." So I did. Twenty dollars was a lot of money for me then.

I was able to save a decent amount of money from my jobs, and it came in handy at times. After my father and mother divorced, there was a lengthy period of time when I didn't go to the family dentist. Eventually I had to get caught up, and I accumulated a bill of more than $200 after a few visits. At one of my appointments with Dr. Fritz Morris, he told me Dad hadn't paid my bill. I had about $300 in my savings account, so I was able to pay it myself.

I also was able to cover my tuition at Butler. When the time came to register for classes before my freshman year, I asked my mother if she would write a check for me, and I would pay her back later. She did, but just before I was ready to drive over to campus and register for classes, I received a check in the mail for $200 from my State Fair work. The tuition was $195, and I had an additional $5 in fees, so I just signed my name on the back of the fair check and returned the blank check to Mom.

I found work in college, too. During my freshman year, my mother told me they needed people to work at the Ayres warehouse at 10th and Capitol sorting Christmas packages for delivery. I was hired for 85 cents an hour. I would go home in the afternoon after my last class and study for a while, then report for work at 5:00 p.m. During the Christmas season, I had to report at 4:00 p.m. and stay as late as midnight or one a.m.

Because of lack of sleep, I often dozed off during my 8:00 a.m. Psychology class at Butler. That was the only time I ever fell asleep in a class, and it was only from November until the end of December.

Later during my time at Butler, I got a job with the *Times,* reporting to its downtown office on weekend nights to take the results of football and basketball games over the telephone from high school correspondents.

I also worked for the student paper at Butler, the *Collegian.* That wasn't a paying position, but it provided practical experience for the sports writing career I was considering at the time. I reported on various sports, but never baseball because I was on the team.

I worked my way up to editor my senior year, but had to quit because I was offered a chance to work for the mayor, Alex Clark. I wrote some of his minor speeches and researched answers to questions he took for his Sunday evening radio show on WIRE, "Ask the Mayor." People would write letters asking about various issues around the city. Mr. Clark wasn't big on details, so it was my job to do the leg work. I'd go to the Sanitation Board, for example, and talk to the people there to get an answer to a question, then give it to him to read on the air. I was paid roughly $100 per month, which was a crucial amount of money for me.

○

My Army hitch took me out of the work force, but I began preparing to reenter it shortly before I was to be discharged. I was getting the *Indianapolis Star* in the mail every day at Fort Sheridan, and one day around the first of November in 1956—a month before I would become a civilian again—I read that the Indianapolis Indians ticket manager was leaving the organization.

I called J. R. Townsend Sr., whom I knew from Junior League baseball and regarded as a mentor. He was the Director of Parks and Recreation in Indianapolis and also observed Big Ten football officials on autumn weekends. He invited me at least once every fall to observe the officials with him at Purdue games, so we got to know one another very well. He was acquainted with Frank McKinney Sr., who was the volunteer Chairman of the Board of the Indians. I asked Mr. Townsend if he would call Mr. McKinney on my behalf. He called me back a week or two later and said I had an appointment with Mr. McKinney.

After I returned home from the Army in December, I dressed up and put on a necktie to go see Mr. McKinney in his Fidelity Bank office. The interview only lasted 15 or 20 minutes, but he wrote a note on a small slip of paper for the general manager of the Indians, Ray Johnston.

Mr. McKinney asked me to go meet Al Schlensker, who was the corporate secretary of the Indians. He just wanted him to be in the loop on any possible personnel changes. I drove out to see Mr. Schlensker at National Liquors and then took the note to Johnston. And just like that, I was hired. If you are a general manager and the chairman of the board tells you to hire someone, it's done.

I was overjoyed. My passion for baseball and for working had merged fortuitously and quickly into a full-time job.

I started work for the Indians on January 2, 1957, a Wednesday. The pay was only $350 per month, but it was a lot more than I was making in the Army, and I received the added bonus of meeting my future wife. Judy Whybrew was a part-time employee in the Indians ticket department, working on game days and occasionally when the team was on the road. This was her summer job while studying at Indiana University until she graduated in June of 1958 with a degree in elementary education. Judy enjoyed working for my predecessor, Marge Smyth, and was disappointed when Marge was fired by Ray

Johnston at the end of the 1956 season. Judy was still getting over the loss of her good friend when I took over, but a mutual friend told her I was "OK." Judy's ticket experience was helpful to "rookie Max," and before long we became friends. And then we became more than that. We began to date in the summer of '57—our first night out together, appropriately, was spent seeing *Damn Yankees* at Starlight Musicals. We were married on December 20, 1958.

My first task for the Indians was to contact the people who had bought season tickets in previous years and try to get them renewed. Then I'd try to get new people on board as well. I had the advantage of knowing a lot of people in Indianapolis, and tried to use that to the Indians' advantage.

I was the ticket manager for two years. Then sometime early in my third year, the 1959 season, the publicity director resigned and I was asked to do both jobs. The Indians had won the Junior World Series in 1956, when future Yankees star Roger Maris batted .293 during the regular season and hit two home runs in one Series game. But despite finishing with a 92 – 62 record and sweeping Rochester in four games for the championship, attendance had been flat throughout the season. The team had losing records the following two seasons, so it was only getting worse.

I was well aware of our precarious financial situation, and I was accustomed to working hard. My journalism background at Butler was good preparation for being the publicity director, so I felt confident I could do both jobs.

I didn't get an increase in salary, just twice the work. But I had never minded working harder and longer than most people, and this was a great opportunity for me to establish myself with the organization. When the team was on the road, I would come into the office at 9:00 a.m. and leave at 5:00 p.m. On the days of home games, I would come in at 9:00 a.m. and stay all day without ever leaving the office. I ate cold cuts for lunch and dinner.

I stayed after the game to compile the stats by hand, then typed them up and handed them out to media members. I also called the local radio stations and recorded a "voicer" for them to air that summarized the game. And, I wrote all the press releases, both on the games and any other newsworthy items related to the franchise.

Later, I was designated the business manager. And then early in the 1961 season, when I was 28 years old, Indians president "Ownie" Bush said, "You should consider yourself the general manager. You're already doing the work of that title." He didn't like to get involved in the business side of things, so he left it all to me. I did get an increase in salary that time, although I don't remember how much.

Still, money wasn't the driving force for me. I was working in baseball, and that was enough. ●

THE PUBLIC GOES TO BAT

B y joining the Indianapolis Indians in 1957, I missed all the excitement of the fall of 1955, when the franchise came close to leaving Indianapolis. Cleveland Indians owner Ryan Ellis had purchased the franchise from Frank McKinney Sr. and Ownie Bush in 1951, but it turned out to be a bad investment for him. Indianapolis won the American Association pennant in 1954, but otherwise struggled to field a competitive team. It finished seventh in an eight-team league in '55, when Ellis claimed to have lost more than $150,000.

McKinney and Robert Kirby, chairman of the Chamber of Commerce athletic committee, went to Cleveland to talk with general manager Hank Greenberg and were told Indianapolis would lose its franchise if a local person or group didn't step up to purchase the team. Greenberg claimed to have offers from three other cities who wanted to purchase the franchise, so something needed to be done quickly.

The city had about one month, until November 26, to come up with 75 percent of the $160,000 required to purchase the team, make repairs at Victory Field, and finance the next season. McKinney took his stock-purchasing plan to the public on November 4, and on November 10, order blanks began appearing in the three local newspapers—on

Page 1—accompanied by a story detailing the do-or-die nature of the campaign. Order forms were later placed in grocery stores, factories, and other points in the city.

Each share of stock cost $10, with a minimum purchase of 10 shares and a maximum purchase of 100. I was away in the Army at the time and read about the offering in the *Star*, but couldn't scrounge up $10 to buy even one share.

The newspapers further supported the drive with consistent news articles, columns, editorials, and editorial cartoons that encouraged people to save the Indians for Indianapolis. They also published the names of everyone who bought stock, which made it a competition of sorts. A man might go to work in the morning and say to a friend, "Hey, did you see my name in the paper for buying a share of Indians stock? When are you going to get some?" One former Indians batboy from 1937, Hank Clouse, who owned a photo studio, even offered to shoot a family portrait for anyone who purchased at least one share.

"I can never forget what it meant to me when I was a kid, and I wouldn't want the kids of today to be denied the opportunities that baseball offers," he told an *Indianapolis News* reporter.

Another newspaper photograph showed members of an east side coffee club sitting in a restaurant. A painted sign on the wall listed the members of the club and invited everyone to join for the entry fee of at least one share of stock.

The public responded beautifully to the spirited drive. Ultimately, the Indians raised nearly $205,000 from 6,672 shareholders. I have no doubt some of the shareholders weren't baseball fans, they just saw the Indians as a community asset worth preserving, similar to the symphony orchestra or the public library.

Many shares were purchased by parents for their children. Years later, we devoted endless hours to finding shareholders during a reverse split. Many weren't even aware they owned shares. We didn't have addresses for many of them. Some people had purchased shares in the names of their children but didn't inform them, or the children forgot.

Fast forward to modern times after we had become a profitable operation and publications such as the *Indianapolis Business Journal* published articles on our financial status. People saw that and called to say they remember having bought a share of stock many years earlier and wanted to redeem their certificates. We had to tell them we had tried to reach them, but the letters had come back because of a wrong address. Shareholders have an obligation to inform companies in which they own stock of address changes and if they had missed the deadline to participate in the reverse split we weren't able to restore their position. Their shares no longer had monetary value.

We didn't have many complaints, because most of the shareholders realized they hadn't done their part to stay in touch with the team. Many of them framed their original certificates as mementos and let it go at that.

Stock in the Indians is not available for purchase today unless it is bought from an existing shareholder. We have an annual buyback program, so if a shareholder wants to liquidate his or her stock, we'll send a check for the buyback price. We had a reverse split of five-to-one, so five shares became the equivalent of one. That original share price of $10 would be the equivalent of $50 today.

The original stockholders' purchases turned out to be a great investment. More importantly, they saved the Indians for Indianapolis, and saved a future career for me. ●

Ownie Bush, shown with infielder Marv Staehle, preferred to be photographed from his right to hide the impact of the surgery on his left cheekbone.

OWEN J. BUSH

O wen Joseph Bush was well-known in the baseball world, and by a variety of names. He grew up on the east side of Indianapolis as Owen. As an adult, most people in the baseball world called him "Donie," a nickname that resulted from a telegrapher's error. In Indianapolis, however, we called him "Ownie" after he became the Indians' owner and president.

He remained active in professional baseball from 1905, when he began his playing career in the minors as a teenager, until he passed away in 1972 at age 84. He was an outstanding shortstop, the leader in putouts and assists during a major-league playing career that lasted from 1908 – 23. He wasn't a great hitter (.250 career average), but he was among the very best at drawing walks and stealing bases. He led the American League in runs scored (112) in 1917 and scored more than 100 runs in a season four times.

Bush played all but his final two seasons with Detroit, where he was a longtime teammate of Ty Cobb. He once told me Cobb was "the best ballplayer I ever saw, but I had no respect for him personally."

Bush and Cobb had quite a lot in common, though. Both were small (Bush was 5-foot-6 and about 130 pounds), both made the most of their abilities with aggressiveness, and both were stubborn.

Bush proved that while managing, too. He directed seven teams in the minors and Majors, including two stops with the Indians, from 1924 – 26 and again from 1943 – 44. His most notable managing experience came with Pittsburgh in 1927.

The Pirates won 94 games that season, but had to face a New York Yankees team regarded by many as the greatest ever assembled in the World Series. These were the "Murderers Row" Yankees who finished 110 – 44 and had a roster that included seven future Hall of Famers. Babe Ruth hit a record 60 home runs that season, and Lou Gehrig batted .373 and drove in a record 175 runs.

The Pirates' roster featured five future Hall of Famers, but Bush benched one of them, outfielder Kiki Cuyler, late in the season and throughout the World Series.

Cuyler, who batted .309 that season, reportedly was angry over being moved from third to second in the batting order and let it affect his effort. Bush fined him $50 for not trying to break up a double play by sliding in to second base in a game on August 9. Cuyler played the next day, but only appeared a few times after that as a pinch-hitter. He didn't play at all in the World Series. Bush used a pinch-hitter on five occasions in the Series, but didn't call for Cuyler.

Bush caught hell from Pirates fans for not playing Cuyler, but stood firm. He told me many years later he had benched Cuyler because the outfielder "rainbowed" his throws from the outfield, which allowed baserunners to advance on fly balls. He also once told Fred Russell, the sports editor of the Nashville Banner, that Cuyler had challenged him after Bush admonished him for one of his looping throws had allowed an opponent to advance to second base on a fly ball and then score on a single.

"Won't you ever learn to throw the ball low?" Bush recalled saying to Cuyler as he entered the dugout.

"If you don't like the way I play, get somebody else," Cuyler responded, according to Bush.

"I will," Bush said.

It was a battle of two stubborn men, and both lost out on that occasion. Cuyler went on to play 11 more successful seasons for the Cubs, Reds, and Dodgers. He died of a heart attack in 1951 and was inducted into the Hall of Fame in 1968. Bush went on to other managing jobs after resigning from the Pirates two years later. He had continued to live on Indianapolis's east side during the offseasons, and had become a close friend of a bank teller, Frank E. McKinney Sr. McKinney had a deep love for baseball and Bush admired McKinney's agile business mind, so it only followed they would become friends.

The friendship grew as McKinney's banking career expanded. Bush eventually insisted that the Democrat Party support McKinney for County Treasurer, and McKinney was elected to the office that provided lucrative commissions for collection of delinquent taxes, a significant boost for McKinney's business and political career.

Bush benefitted from his friend's loyalty as he was included in various deals initiated by McKinney. They included beer and liquor distribution, broadcasting, and baseball.

They, along with Boston Red Sox owner Tom Yawkey, purchased the Louisville Colonels minor-league team in 1938. McKinney and Bush sold their shares to Yawkey in 1940, and a year later bought the Indianapolis Indians from Norm Perry. Bush managed the team in 1943, but had to give up that position early the following season because of ill health. He and McKinney sold the franchise to the Cleveland Indians in 1952, and four years later helped lead the effort to transform it to a community-owned franchise via a public stock offering and repurchase of the franchise from Cleveland.

Bush held executive positions with the Indians throughout all the ownership changes, and was the team president when I joined the franchise in 1957. He designated me the general manager in 1961 and gave me the freedom to do my job because he didn't want to concern himself with the business side of baseball. He limited his role to the players, managers, and won-loss record. He expected others to generate the sales of tickets, advertising and sponsorships, and worry about profits. Although he had many friends throughout Indianapolis, he never offered to help the front office staff make contacts that could have improved the company's bottom line.

I had a good professional relationship with him. The only conflict we encountered with any consistency was over playing in marginal weather conditions. He would telephone me many times on the day of a game when the weather was threatening to suggest it be postponed. If rain was falling at his east side home, or if the radio and television stations were predicting an overnight freeze, I could count on hearing from him. He was taking a short-term view, thinking how the weather might affect that day's attendance as well as his personal comfort. I was seeing the bigger picture and wanting to avoid playing excessive doubleheaders in July and August when player fatigue could become a factor for our team. If we lost a game he advised me to postpone, he would likely remind me of it the following morning. If we won, he said nothing about it.

Bush stayed out of the public eye as much as possible. He lived with his mother in the east side home in which he had grown up after returning to Indianapolis to work with the Indians, and continued living in that house by himself—he never married or had children—until he passed away.

He shunned publicity, in any form. Dick Mittman, a local sportswriter, often tried to get Ownie to talk about his baseball memories, but was always rebuffed.

"Talk to someone else," Bush would say. "I'm bad copy."

Bush and I never had an argument over his authority, as frequently happens when a young executive is working with an older one who is about to retire. By the late 1960s, he was content merely to go to spring training, be with old friends, have a few beers, and talk baseball. He didn't do much in the office. He would come in about nine a.m. most days. By ten, he would go to the refrigerator and open a beer and begin sipping. He would go to lunch with friends and then either go home or return for a couple more hours. It was a comfortable situation for him because he didn't have to concern himself with the day-to-day business operations.

I was a loyal subordinate to him. I even drove out to San Diego with Judy in 1963 in our six-cylinder Buick to attend the winter baseball meetings when he was honored as the Minor League King of Base-ball—an award I later received in 1997. I drove his crown, cape, and scepter back so he could fly home without having to deal with them.

His ending with the Indians was unpleasant for everyone. He re-tired at the age of 81 in 1969 with a letter to the board of directors in which he expressed disagreement with the actions board chairman Lou Hensley and I had taken in December to reorganize the front office.

"I just can't agree on some matters with Hensley and Schumacher," he wrote, in a statement that appeared in the newspapers.

That was an unfortunate way for our professional relationship to end. He had promoted me to general manager in 1961 and we general-ly had gotten along well. I accepted his unique status with the franchise and was happy to do whatever was assigned to me. I also was in no hurry to replace him as the lead executive. He was 81 years old, and obviously wasn't going to stay in the job much longer.

Ownie Bush (middle) won the King of Baseball award in 1963. He is pictured with (clockwise from lower left) Johnny Hutchings, Bob Weimer, Art Wright, Ray Johnston, Max Schumacher, and Bob Kirby.

His role with the Indians had greatly diminished in recent years because of health issues. He had been struck by cancer, and part of his left jaw had been removed as a result. He rarely appeared in the office and didn't like to be out in public. Most of the photographs of him from that era show him from the right side.

The Indians had lost $35,000 in 1968 and were in a severe financial crisis, so a practical decision was made to drop his salary from the payroll. He stated that was not his reason for retiring, but he never did specify his disagreements with Hensley and me.

The board tried to treat him fairly. He was given the title of team president and told he was welcome to remain involved with the franchise, but he declined. It's often difficult for executives, managers, and players to get out of the game gracefully, and that turned out to be true for Ownie as well.

The White Sox weren't our major-league affiliate at the time, but they hired him as a scout so he could stay in baseball and get together with old friends. He was at their spring-training site in March of 1972 when he became ill and had to return to Indianapolis, and died later that month.

He was a large enough figure in baseball that both his retirement and death were front-page headlines in the Indianapolis newspapers and were reported throughout the nation. He's still the "biggest" baseball figure to come out of Indianapolis, and had a major impact on the Indians. ◈

Max tried, but couldn't convince Ownie Bush to have more patience with Harmon Killebrew.

HARMON KILLEBREW AND ROGER MARIS

Harmon Killebrew played briefly for the Indianapolis Indians in 1958, having been optioned from the Washington Senators in May. We were affiliated with the White Sox at the time, and needed a third baseman. Ownie Bush was friends with an executive in the Senators' front office, so he convinced him to send Killebrew to us. Strange as it sounds today, Washington didn't have a Triple-A team at the time. That was an era when some major-league teams had two Triple-A affiliates, and the Dodgers even had three—in Montreal, St. Paul and Spokane. Today, major-league teams must have one—and only one—Triple-A and Double-A affiliate.

Harmon was 24 years old when he came to the Indians. He had played sporadically in the Majors for five seasons by then and had led the Southern Association in home runs in 1957. He played in 13 games for the Senators early in the '58 season but batted just .194, so they were anxious to send him to us for more seasoning.

You could never meet a nicer guy. I was working in the ticket office at the time, and the players came through there to pick up their mail on their way to the clubhouse. Harmon began getting all these cases of Wheaties cereal boxes. Apparently General Mills saw him as a promising player they might want to endorse someday, so they kept shipping cereal to him. He received far more boxes than any one man could eat, so he eventually asked if I'd like them. As a young man on a tight budget, I said sure.

The Wheaties didn't help Harmon's play, though. He was batting .215 with just two home runs after 38 games with the Indians, so Ownie Bush gave up on him. I tried to reason with Ownie, and showed him stats that proved Harmon was starting to come around, but Ownie just wouldn't buy it. His mind was made up. He finally convinced the White Sox and Washington to get Killebrew out of Indianapolis. I remember Ownie saying, "Get me a player who can play!" So we got Stan Roseboro instead. He was a journeyman minor leaguer who hit just .257 for us and had no power.

Harmon broke through the following season, hitting 42 homers in the Majors for the Senators, and went on to a Hall of Fame career in which he hit 573 home runs. Few would have predicted that during his brief time with Indianapolis.

Roger Maris starred for the Indianapolis Indians in 1956, the season before Max arrived.

Killebrew's story was somewhat reminiscent of that of Roger Maris, although the Indians didn't give up on Maris. He played for the Indians in 1956, the season before I arrived. He was 21 years old and the veteran of parts of three seasons in Cleveland's minor-league system at that time. He hit just .083 over the first eight exhibition games, and wondered aloud about his chances of sticking.

"I just hope [manager Kerby Farrell] doesn't give up on me too quickly," he said. "I'll start hitting if he sticks with me. And if I don't make Triple A this year, I may never make it."

Maris improved enough to catch on with the team, but started the season slowly at the plate. He wasn't playing well in the outfield, either. Cleveland's management was pressuring Farrell to send him down to the Double-A affiliate in Tulsa, where he had hit .233 the previous season. But Farrell went the other direction. He moved Maris from left to right, drilled him endlessly on his fielding and throwing skills, convinced him to choke up on the bat and committed to playing him in 10 consecutive games despite the Indians' deep outfield at the time.

The cumulative effect was that Maris improved as the season went along and finished it a completely different player than he had been at the start. He hit .293 with 17 home runs and 75 RBI as the Indians won the Junior World Series with a sweep over the International League champion Rochester. Maris was one of the leaders of the team's strong finish, and had two home runs and seven RBI in Game Two of the championship series.

Five years later, after being traded twice in the Majors, Maris broke Babe Ruth's 34-year-old home run record by hitting 61 for the Yankees in 1961.

It's odd to think he had nearly suffered the same fate as Killebrew with the Indians. Thanks to a patient and persistent Kirby Farrell, Maris at least was able to finish one season with the franchise. It's a shame Killebrew didn't have the same opportunity. ●

Johnny Hutchings, honored during his retirement ceremony in 1951, was one of the most popular Indianapolis Indians of his era.

JOHNNY HUTCHINGS

O f all the men who have worn the Indianapolis Indians uniform, Johnny Hutchings might rank as the most sympathetic figure. He was as beloved by the fans of his era as any player in franchise history to that point, but ultimately his love was rejected by Ownie Bush. ● Hutchings's career as a professional pitcher lasted from 1935 – 51. He pitched for the Indians between 1942 and 1951, between callups to the Boston Braves of the National League. His overall record with the Indians was 52 – 34, while his major-league record with Cincinnati and the Braves was 12 – 18.

He was known in the Majors for his unique pickoff attempts at second base. Rather than turning and throwing the ball, he merely flipped it sideways with one quick motion of his right wrist. His manager in Boston, Casey Stengel, had him demonstrate in clinics.

Although Hutchings compiled a winning record for the Indians, his popularity stemmed largely from his sense of humor, both as a player in the 1940s and a coach in the 1950s. He often made a dramatic show of pretending to trip over the third-baseline on his way to the dugout. He made crowd-pleasing hand gestures toward umpires from behind his back from the coaching box. He would take a big gulp of water in the dugout and spray it onto the field. And, as one newspaper reporter wrote, he could "mimic anybody who moved."

As a kid in the '40s, I once watched him genuinely trip while trying to field a topped ball rolling down the third baseline. The third baseman made the play, so Hutchings just continued somersaulting all the way to the dugout.

No wonder the fans loved him.

His weight contributed to his persona. He played at about 250 pounds, but ballooned past 330 as a coach. The local sportswriters often referred to him as "jovial" or a "big jolly fellow" or "rotund and riotous"—or, simply, "exceedingly popular." He further endeared himself to the local fans by moving his wife and four children to Indianapolis in 1948, and continuing to live there.

He was serious about wanting to become a manager, though, so he left Indianapolis in 1959 to manage a Class D team in Clinton, Iowa of the Midwest League to gain experience. After finishing second in the voting for Manager of the Year, Ownie Bush signed him to a one-year contract to manage the Indians in December of '59.

The backstory to that agreement has never been told, however.

Ownie had offered him the job the previous winter under the condition he lose 100 pounds. Johnny went on a salt-free diet and took off the weight, dropping 105 pounds to 230 according to newspaper reports. Those reports also stated he had lost 55 pounds over the previous six weeks alone, and that his waist size had shrunk from 50 inches to 40.

Johnny's rapid weight loss landed him in the hospital not long before he signed his contract to manage the Indians, but he eventually was pronounced fit enough to work. Ownie Bush told reporters Johnny had been ill and left it at that.

Media members and fans alike greeted the hire enthusiastically, but the timing was all wrong for Johnny. The Indians had ended their affiliation with the White Sox after the '59 season and were an independent team heading into the 1960 season. We eventually signed a limited partnership with Philadelphia, but the Phillies' Triple-A team in Buffalo had right of first refusal on all players. That meant the Indians essentially would be playing with Double-A talent against Triple-A competition.

No manager was going to win with that kind of talent, especially a rookie manager. A run of injuries early in the season didn't help either. The Indians lost 10 consecutive games in June and fell into last place, so Ownie decided to make a change. Johnny was offered the face-saving opportunity to resign, but he refused, believing he had done the job as well as could be expected under the circumstances.

He was going to have to be fired, then, but not until a business decision was made. The ticket receipts for our July 4 doubleheader and fireworks show indicated the largest crowd of the season was due, so Ownie held off making the announcement to protect the gate.

The Indians won both ends of that doubleheader before 7,769 fans, improving our record to 30 – 49. The article in the *Star,* written immediately after the games, acknowledged rumors that Hutchings was on the "hot seat," but added "it looks now that there is no danger flag-waving."

It waved the following morning. The players had gone to the extreme of signing a petition to express their support for Hutchings, but it didn't help. Ownie pulled the trigger, claiming he thought Johnny lacked managing experience.

Hutchings was extremely disappointed by the decision but handled it professionally. A photograph appeared in the afternoon *News* showing him smiling and hugging his successor, player-coach Ted Beard at the press conference announcing the change, and he was quoted saying he two would remain the "best of friends." One of the newspaper accounts, however, described Johnny as "tearful."

Beard, a 40-year-old outfielder, cut back his playing time after becoming manager. He hit .259 for the season and played in the All-Star game in Denver, contributing a pinch-hit double. The Indians lost their first game under his direction, 11 – 1, falling to Jim Kaat, who went on to pitch 25 major-league seasons. Beard's record for his part of the season wound up 35 – 40, and we finished 65 – 89, one game ahead of last place.

Hutchings still maintained the generous spirit that had made him so popular. He continued to live in Indianapolis and attended Indians games occasionally as a spectator. He stayed involved in baseball, too. He was the lead instructor at a new baseball academy, participated in clinics throughout the city, emceed the opening-day ceremonies for a Little League, participated in an intrasquad game at the end of the 1961 season, performed offseason promotional work for the Indians and was a popular guest speaker at local sports banquets.

He took a job with a beer distributor and settled into a comfortable life. But on April 27, 1963, he died of uremia, a condition that occurs when the kidneys fail and blood becomes poisoned. He was 47 years old.

His passing was front-page news and tributes flowed from the media. Les Koelling, who covered the Indians for the *News*, described Johnny as "the most popular player ever to wear the Indians uniform." Jep Cadou Jr., sports editor of the *Star*, wrote that Hutchings came from an era when there was "still time and room for some levity in baseball, before the moguls drained the game of all its color."

The Indians were ready to raise the banner for winning the pennant in the 1963 season at the time of Hutchings' death, and flew it at half-mast for the first month of the '64 season in his honor. I was proud to be among the pallbearers at his funeral service.

After bringing so much joy to fans, Hutchings' life ended too quickly and unfairly. He had finally gotten his shot at managing, but nobody could have led that 1960 Indians team to a successful season. One year later, we established an affiliation with Cincinnati and won the regular-season championship in the American Association.

One season too late for Johnny. ◉

1961

I was 28 years old when I took over as the Indianapolis Indians' general manager in 1961. My workload actually became a little lighter because I had traded in my two jobs as ticket manager and publicity director for one. But I had a lot to learn. ● We hired Maury Rome, who had handled tickets at various venues around the community, to be a seasonal employee during the baseball season. We also hired Estel Freeman as the publicity director. He had worked at a local television station, Channel 6, and had broadcast Indians game in 1947 with Gene Kelly. When he heard the job was available he applied and became the first person I hired in my new role. He was a good man, and he liked to sell, which was always an asset in my eyes.

Ray Johnston, the previous general manager, had left to become owner of the American Association franchise in Dallas/Ft. Worth. He left me with a great working agreement, although I didn't know the specifics at the time, but little in the way of preparation for what I was about to encounter.

In December of 1960, while I was still the business manager, the baseball winter meetings were conducted in Louisville, Kentucky. I had never attended, and it would have been a great opportunity to get acquainted with other general managers and league procedures, but Ray never suggested that I go. As a result, I felt as if I was playing from behind from the beginning, and for a long time afterward.

I was in for a pleasant surprise, though.

We became the Triple-A affiliate of the Cincinnati Reds that season in the American Association, after a one-season deal with Philadelphia. The Reds' other Triple-A affiliate was the Jersey City Jerseys of the International League. That team consisted of players from the Havana Sugar Kings, who had traveled to the United States from Cuba the previous season for a series of games against International League teams. The franchise moved after the tour and became the Jersey City franchise in 1961.

During spring training, the Reds' leading minor-league prospects were divided between Jersey City and the Indians. As the Jersey City officials and I watched them play, the Jersey City general manager said, "You may see some of these good players in your lineup this spring, but we'll have them when we break camp." I wasn't sure what he was talking about, but I was new so I didn't say much.

We then had a meeting at the end of spring training to determine how players would be assigned. There, Phil Seghi, the Reds farm director, pulled out his wallet and removed a folded piece of paper he'd kept for several months. He said, "These are the players who were promised to Indianapolis last fall when the agreement was made."

The list included nearly all of the Reds' best Triple-A players.

That's why I said Ray Johnston left me a good deal. He hadn't told me about the arrangement with the Reds and Jersey City, just like he didn't tell me about a lot of other things, but it provided us with numerous quality players. I'll always be grateful to Phil Seghi for his integrity, too. It would have been easy for him to forget about that piece of paper in his wallet and send those players to Jersey City. He caught a lot of grief from the Jersey City front office, but he did the honorable thing and lived up to an agreement I didn't know anything about.

I also was lucky to have Ellis "Cot" Deal as our manager in my rookie season as GM. He was new to Indianapolis and needed a place to stay, so he lived in my mother's basement for a month or two. She eventually asked him to leave, however, because he smoked. My father had been a heavy smoker so she probably had breathed enough second-hand smoke for one lifetime.

Cot (his nickname referred to his cotton-like hair color as a young kid growing up in Oklahoma City) and I became good friends regardless of that mishap. He was more than just a field manager, he had a feel for things in the front office and was a great help to me. He'd come up to my office after nearly every game and ask about the attendance—and a lot of nights it wasn't very good. Best of all, he was a good baseball manager.

The season began with plenty of drama for me, not all of it on the field. After winning our opener, the next two games were postponed because of snow. This was on April 16 and 17, mind you, a rare storm for that time of year. Cot conducted practices inside Butler Fieldhouse on the basketball court and outside on the university's cinder track to help the players stay as sharp as possible under the circumstances.

Cot Deal was manager of the Indianapolis Indians in 1961.

We made up those games with doubleheaders, the first one a day later that was televised locally on Channel 4. I watched the first game at the park, went home, watched the second game on TV, and then took Judy to the hospital to give birth to our second child, Brian.

One of the highlights for me that season was pitching batting practice. Not many general managers can make that claim, but Cot asked me to do it, knowing I had played in college and in the Army. I was flattered to be asked and believed I could perform well. I didn't do it before every game, but I did it for several home games. I had a good, strong arm and I could locate the ball well, so I was what everybody was looking for in a batting practice pitcher.

The purpose was mostly to build confidence in the hitters. Ironically, the guy who hit me the best was Harry Anderson. He'd launch majestic drives well beyond the right field fence onto Harding Street. He didn't fare as well against real pitching, though, batting just .217 in 89 at-bats with three home runs. The only other time I pitched batting practice was in 1968, when Hal McRae was rehabbing an injury and stayed behind when the team was on the road.

Fortunately, we had some players who hit when it counted. We won the American Association pennant that season, and one of the primary reasons was because of a trade I made early in April that Cot had recommended to me.

We had two right-handed hitting outfielders, Carlos Bernier and Joe Gaines, early in the season. Bernier, a 34-year-old veteran with a bit of a checkered reputation, was hitting .271. Gaines, a 24-year-old prospect, also was off to a good start.

They were splitting time, and we needed to trade one of them to allow the other to play full time and flourish. I consulted with Cot and he said if we kept Gaines he would get better because the pressure on him would be reduced, but if we kept Bernier he probably would get worse because he felt like he had it made. Bernier, then, was the one to move.

At that time, I would get the minor-league batting averages from a news bureau in Chicago. The stats were a week old, but still were better than nothing. I learned that two or three of the outfielders for Hawaii in the Pacific Coast League were batting under .200, so I called their general manager and offered Bernier in a trade. We owned his contract and had put $2,500 into it, with the hope of making money off it. I asked for $3,500 or a player to be named later. But I said if you don't want to pay the $3,500, in the fall I want Bernier back, because I thought we might need him in 1962.

It worked out beautifully. Gaines was a perfect gentleman, a good teammate, and wound up leading the team with a .315 average. He got better as the season progressed, as Cot Deal had predicted. Bernier went to Hawaii and led the PCL with a .351 batting average.

By the end of the season, they had changed general managers in Hawaii. The new one said he thought they owed us a player to be named later. I said, no, you have to send Bernier back to us or cash. We argued for a while but he checked around and finally agreed to send us the $3,500. So, we turned a profit of $1,000 on the contract, which was significant for us at the time.

We also made a good trade with Syracuse in July. We sent pitcher Mike Cuellar and infielder-outfielder Larry Raines in return for infielder Chet Boak and outfielder Lamar Jacobs. They proved to be valuable utility players and pinch-hitters, batting .300 and .292, respectively. Cuellar went on to an outstanding major-league career, most of it with Baltimore, and was inducted into the Hall of Fame in 1983. He hadn't shown that talent with us, though, and didn't stick with a major-league team until 1964.

The regular season was a grand success. The Indians set a franchise attendance record on July 25 when 19,966 fans showed up for a game against Denver that was sponsored by Standard Grocery. Our third baseman, Cliff Cook, was voted the American Association's Most Valuable Player after hitting .311 with 32 home runs. Shortstop Chico Ruiz was voted Rookie of the Year after batting .272 and leading the league with 44 stolen bases. Pitcher Don Rudolph finished 18 – 9, and catcher-first baseman Don Pavletich hit .295 with 22 home runs.

Best of all, we won the American Association pennant with an 86 – 64 record. The league was down to six teams, but a playoff series between the first- and fourth-place teams and the second- and third-place teams was conducted to determine who would play the International League champion in the Junior World Series. We were matched against the Houston Buffs, who had snuck into fourth place for the final playoff spot on the last day of the season and finished 73 – 77.

Hurricane Carla had swept through the Gulf of Mexico shortly before the playoffs began, so all the games had to be played in Indianapolis. That seemed like a great deal for us. Houston had finished 13 games behind the Indians in the standings, and now we would get to play every game in Indianapolis.

It didn't work out as we hoped. Houston won the series 4 – 1, playing as the home team for the final two games of the series on our field. They won the final game, 6 – 0, before just 1,738 fans, an anticlimactic finish to an otherwise great season.

The outcome left our fans feeling empty and angry, losing to a fourth-place team in a playoff series after such a great season. It was the 19th time in the 26-year history of the playoff format—which had been instituted to stimulate attendance in cities where the team had fallen out of the playoff race—that the regular-season champion had been eliminated before the Junior World Series. In this instance, Houston had momentum from its late charge to earn a playoff berth on the final day while the Indians had coasted to a six-game lead over sec-

A capacity crowd at Bush Stadium was always a beautiful sight to behold.

ond-place Louisville in the final standings. Throw in a little overconfi-dence on our part, and the result was an upset.

The season had been so enjoyable that the Indianapolis Chamber of Commerce hurriedly organized a "Player Appreciation Night." It was announced on September 9 and was to be conducted on the 16th. Local merchants were invited to donate 25 of something to be given to each of the players. The hope was to get 25 merchants or individuals to do so, but 32 responded. The hope also was to have the night held in con-junction with a playoff game, but we had to go to the backup plan—an intrasquad game—because of our playoff elimination.

Former Brooklyn Dodgers pitcher Carl Erskine, who lived an hour north of Indianapolis in Anderson, and Cloyd Boyer, the Indians pitch-ing coach, teamed up to lead a 5 – 1 victory over a team led by out-fielder Ted Beard and former pitcher and manager Johnny Hutchings. Only 479 fans paid to watch the game, but that anyone at all showed up was a testament to the affection people had for that team. The ticket proceeds were divided among the players.

Apparently Cot Deal was impressed with my batting practice pitch-ing, because he let me pitch a couple of innings in the game. It was a fun way to end my "rookie season" as a general manager. It had been a tremendous learning experience for me—and the lessons continued after the season ended.

Late in the season, I was able to negotiate the sale of second baseman Jim Snyder's contract to Minnesota. Twins owner Calvin Griffith flew to one of our games in either Houston or Dallas for a look at Snyder before approving my asking price of $25,000. Snyder's major-league career didn't pan out—he played in three games for the Twins at the end of the '61 season, 12 in 1962, and 26 in '64—but I'll always remember Snyder fondly. The $25,000 we received for his contract turned out to be our approximate profit for that season. He wasn't done with the Indians, though, as he returned to manage Indianapolis in 1976.

I had less luck trying to unload another contract.

Spec Richardson, the newly-appointed general manager of Hous-ton's major-league expansion franchise that was to begin play the following season, watched the playoff games with me. During our time together, I tried to convince him to buy Len Johnston's contract after the season. Johnston was 32 years old at the time but had batted .297 for us during the regular season and I made the case to Spec that he could help an expansion franchise because of his experience.

My argument was foiled by Buffs pitcher Dave Giusti, who was headed toward a lengthy major-league career. Giusti struck out Johnston four times in one of the games, so my sales pitch died along with our playoff hopes.

While Giusti helped spoil that hope, another plan went awry because of my own ignorance.

I told the players late in the season we would buy them rings if they won the regular-season pennant. Once that had been accomplished, I had them measured for the rings. You might not think a Triple-A pennant is a big deal, but many men play their entire professional career without winning any kind of championship. And many Triple-A players don't reach the Majors, so that represents their ultimate achievement in baseball. Winning a championship at that level means something to them.

I placed "championship rings" on the end-of-season board meeting agenda, but hadn't discussed it prior to that with board chairman Frank McKinney Sr. He considered it an unnecessary expense and quickly shot it down. The board supported him with a "no" vote.

The players didn't let me forget it. Whenever I would see members of that team in later years when they were playing or managing for other teams, they often would ask, "Hey, where are our rings?!" Pavletich loved to needle me about it most of all.

It was a rookie mistake from which I learned a valuable lesson: don't make major decisions without first getting approval from the board, particularly those that add to expenses.

We faced further disappointments in the offseason. Cot Deal, who had been voted Manager of the Year, left to join his friend Harry Craft, who had managed the Buffs in 1961 and was taking over Houston's expansion franchise in the National League the following season.

We also lost our one-season affiliation with the Reds. They were wrapping up their National League pennant when our season ended, and asked Ownie Bush and me to come over for a meeting.

We rode over in Ownie's Cadillac, only to find out the Reds were demanding a new working agreement from us. The previous season we had paid a maximum of $900 per month of every player's contract if his salary was equal to or greater than that amount. The Reds wanted us to pay varying amounts of each contract the following season, depending on the player's talent level—as much as $1,500 per month for the best prospects.

I left the room to take a long distance call during the meeting. When I returned, Ownie told me of the plan and said the Reds were claiming our share of the contracts would come out about the same in the long run. I might have been new to the job, but I wasn't that naïve or lacking in elementary math skills. I applied the numbers of their plan to our previous season's roster and figured we would have had to pay $40,000 more in player salaries—a sum that would have crippled us financially.

The Reds were playing the San Francisco Giants that night. Ownie left the game early to go see a friend who had a Budweiser distributorship in Brookville, Indiana. He was really angry by then because he realized after talking with me that the Reds had lied to him about the projected expenses. I stayed to watch the game, but by the seventh inning, nobody from the Reds had come to see me to discuss the deal any further.

Phil Seghi finally came by and told me Reds president Bill DeWitt thought the deal was equitable. Period. He wasn't interested in hearing my side of the argument. They had an ace in the hole because San Diego had a well-funded minor-league franchise, so the Reds had gone into the meeting knowing they didn't need us any longer, pennant or not.

A day or two later, Ownie and I called the Chicago White Sox. They wanted us to come back to them, and offered a deal that would require us to pay only $800 per month for each contract. So, we came out ahead financially. And it turned out we did just as well on the field, too. ●

FRED HOPKE

A player can help a winning team in a variety of ways. Fred Hopke made most of his contributions in the locker room. ● Hopke was among those players who aren't quite good enough to play at the highest level. He never got a call-up to the Majors, but played 10 minor-league seasons, including one for the Indianapolis Indians in 1961 as a left-handed backup first baseman. He batted just .225 in 213 at-bats, mostly as a pinch-hitter.

His primary role was to warm up pitchers in the bullpen. Midway through the season, our manager, Cot Deal, asked me to purchase a left-handed catcher's mitt to help him with that duty. They aren't that easy to get, because few catchers at professional levels are left-handed.

Despite his limitations as a player, Fred was one of the team's most popular players because of his sense of humor and positive attitude. He was elected the judge of our clubhouse "Kangaroo Court" that passed out fines for infractions such as missing a signal during a game or being late for batting practice. It was an idea Cot brought with him from his earlier baseball stops.

The fines were minimal, usually between $10 and $25, but sometimes players would stand "trial" to appeal their case. Fred would listen patiently while the other players were seated nearby. Usually, the accused's appeal resulted in the fine being doubled while the other players hooted and hollered.

The left-handed catcher's mitt disappeared at the end of the season, never to be seen again. Oh, well. Fred was an honest judge and played an important role on our pennant-winning team.

Fast-forward seven years to 1968, when our manager Don Zimmer was struggling through a losing season. He asked me to suggest a way to improve the team's chemistry and lift everyone's spirits, so I brought up Hopke's Kangaroo Court and described how it had worked.

Zimmer looked me squarely in the eye and said, "We'd have a riot." And that was that. Not all teams are cut out for that kind of thing, with players having to pay fines and taking a lot of kidding. Ironically, those probably are the teams that need it the most. ◉

BACKWARD MARKETING

My predecessor as general manager, Ray Johnston, had begun a strategy of "buyout nights," in which an organization or business could rent the ballpark for a fee and be given a virtually unlimited number of tickets for a game to distribute. I inherited the practice when I took over as general manager in 1961, and got hit with a whopper in my first season. Our biggest buyout game every year had been Standard Grocery Night. Anyone walking through the doors of a Standard grocery store could pick up tickets for free. Many of the tickets would go unused, but some fans took several to distribute to their family members and friends. There was just no way of knowing what to expect.

That season, Standard Grocery Night drew 19,966 fans for a game against Denver in July. It was the largest turnout for an Indians game since a player appreciation night game in July of 1933 had drawn a reported crowd of 22,153. In that game, women and children 16 and under were admitted for free, while men were charged 40 cents.

In our Standard Grocery Night game in 1961, season ticket-holders had access to their seats and all box seats were reserved, but the rest of the park was general admission. Capacity for Victory Field, as it was called then, was about 12,000, so the overflow fans had no place to go but the playing field. Some stood behind ropes along the left field line and others behind ropes across the outfield, 20-feet deep against the wall. Balls hit into the fans were ruled a ground-rule double.

The crowd was unruly at times and the game had to be delayed several times while the grounds crew struggled to keep fans inside the ropes.

We had a major controversy when one of our players, Chet Boak, hit a ball that appeared to go over the billboard in left field for a home run that would have tied the game. I thought the ball cleared the wall and sailed into the parking area outside the stadium. Norm Beplay, our public address announcer, agreed, as did many of the people sitting in the press box. But the umpire, Dave Carabba, said the ball had fallen into the group of fans standing along the wall and ruled it a ground-rule double.

After fans began throwing paper onto the field in protest, Carabba called from the telephone in our dugout to tell Beplay to announce we would have to forfeit the game if the problem continued.

As it turned out, a young boy wearing a baseball glove had trapped the ball as it bounced off the wall, so the call was correct. The general public didn't have access to a replay, however, so most of those 19,000+ fans were bitter as they headed home following our 7 – 4 loss.

I always kept a listed telephone number during my time with the Indians. I rarely received calls from unhappy fans, probably no more than five times, but one of them came the following morning from a woman who told me—repeatedly—that it was difficult enough to beat the other team, but next to impossible to defeat nine players and three umpires.

"I've had enough of this!" she said. "I'm never going to another game!"

I explained to her that I had been in the public address booth and saw the play just as she had seen it, but the call was correct because the boy had trapped the short bounce off the wall and interfered with the play. I also told her our players in the bullpen had a good view of the play and confirmed the umpire was correct. I thought I had clinched the argument with that point, but she refused to believe me and kept repeating her argument that we had been cheated.

I had no problem with Carabba's call, but I wasn't happy with his threat to forfeit the game. The following day, I asked our gatemen to ask him to come up to my office when he arrived at the ballpark. I told him I thought he had overreacted to the crowd's unruliness. When we have that many people in the park, an umpire shouldn't even think about forfeiting the game. That kind of decision would only lead to more problems with the fans and have untold implications on the team.

Dave brought up the fact some of the kids were spinning the lids for the frosted malt containers onto the field, like miniature Frisbees.

"So what?" I said. "Whenever you have a big crowd you're going to have some of that."

"Yeah, but one of them hit me in the butt," he said.

I didn't have much sympathy for him.

Despite the occasional headaches, the buyout nights were successful promotions for us. The Standard Grocery Night was the only time we had to put fans on the field, so the others were less stressful. The cost of a buyout night in 1961 was $5,000, and that fee increased over the years. That was more income than we would have generated from a typical crowd, and we profited in other ways, too. Some of the fans who were given free tickets didn't want to sit in the grandstand, so they anted up extra money to upgrade to a box seat. It also was a great night for concession sales, as everyone in attendance had to have something to eat and drink.

We had numerous buyout nights per season as the years passed. Realtors, life insurance companies and banks all rented the park regularly. The AFL-CIO and United Auto Workers also participated, and competed to draw the largest crowds. We would usually get nearly

15,000 fans on the union nights, but we were able to keep all the fans in the grandstand.

I was never really comfortable with the promotion, though. I considered it "backward marketing." People were becoming accustomed to free tickets. They knew special nights would come around during the season, so they seldom bought full-price tickets. That cheapened the value of the tickets in the long run. It also frustrated season ticket-holders who were annoyed by the rowdier crowd and the difficulty in finding a parking space and dealing with the increased traffic.

I knew all along that I would discontinue the practice when we moved into our new downtown park. At that point, we established a policy of allowing people to bring in their own food and beverage, with glass containers and alcohol prohibited, to sit in the lawn beyond the outfield fence. We had allowed people to do so and sit in the stands at the old park, but that cut into concession sales and wasn't fair to our concessionaire, so we reached a compromise. It enabled fans to save money by bringing in their own food and drinks, although many of them continued to purchase from the concession stands.

Of course, allowing fans to stand in the outfield near the wall or in foul territory wouldn't be permitted today. Even if it were permitted, I would never allow it to happen again. You risk losing control of the crowd, and you can't let that happen.

But those were unforgettable nights, a reflection of a more free-spirited era. And profitable, too. ◉

1962

With Cot Deal having moved on and a new major-league affiliate, we needed a manager. Ownie Bush was respected by the Chicago White Sox for his baseball knowledge, and they approved of his recommendation to hire Luke Appling for the 1962 season. Appling had been a standout shortstop for the White Sox from 1930 – 50, retiring at the age of 43, and would go into the Hall of Fame in 1964.

He had been managing in the minors since 1954, so he was a natural to lead the Indians when we signed the working agreement with the White Sox. He had talent to work with, too. With a completely different roster of White Sox prospects, we won the American Association title again with an 89 – 58 record, 10 games ahead of second-place Omaha.

It was in many ways another magical season. Until the playoffs, at least.

During spring training, Eddie Short, the White Sox general manager, swung deals that exchanged two of his major-league players for three minor leaguers who really helped us: Lou Vassie, Ramon Conde, and Jim Koranda. Conde finished the season with a .353 average. Koranda led the American Association with 103 RBIs while batting .298.

Vassie hit just .243, but was an outstanding defensive infielder, usually playing second base. He had quick hands and turned a double play better than anyone in the minors.

The start of the season was marred by an unfortunate occurrence in which the team's only three African-American players—veteran Harry "Suitcase" Simpson and rookies Tom McCraw and Don Buford—failed to attend the annual preseason banquet. That led some fans to believe they had not been invited because of their race.

Appling had informed the entire team of the "must attend" nature of the banquet several days in advance. Unfortunately, Suitcase Simpson, who by then was 36 years old and a veteran of many hard knocks in a professional career that included eight major-league seasons, advised McCraw and Buford not to attend, saying, "They have to invite you, but they don't really want you to attend."

The incident faded from memory as the players quickly realized there were no racist intentions within the Indians organization, and all three went on to have a productive seasons. Buford played in just 12 games before being sent down to Chicago's Single-A affiliate in the South Atlantic League, which played out of both Savannah, Georgia and Lynchburg, Tennessee. It turned out to be a good move for him, as he hit .323 for a team that finished 92 – 47 and featured several future major-league players. He was back in Indianapolis the following year and had a monster season on his way to a 10-year major-league career that included an All-Star selection in 1971 while playing for the Baltimore Orioles.

Simpson, whose most recent major-league action had come in 1959, batted .279 with 19 home runs and 79 RBI. He still was an outstanding defensive right fielder and became a fan favorite.

McCraw, a first baseman, hit .326 for the Indians despite the interruption of a brief midseason call-up by the White Sox. He won the batting championship because Conde, who batted .353, didn't have enough plate appearances to qualify. Shortstop Al Weis hit .296 and led the league in stolen bases. The Indians did, too, in the team stats, for the fifth consecutive year. Al Worthington led the league's best pitching staff with a 15 – 4 record and a 2.94 earned run average that was second-best in the league.

One of my most memorable players from that team was a relief pitcher, Warren Hacker. He was a 37-year-old veteran of 12 major-league seasons who had gone 3 – 3 for the White Sox the previous season. He was a dominant "closer" before the save statistic became official (in 1969) and did it with an all-business, blue-collar flair.

He threw a side-arm rising fastball and didn't waste pitches by trying to get hitters to swing at balls outside the strike zone. He would quickly shut down opposing rallies while our fans howled with delight.

He was a great competitor, teammate, and gentleman while with the Indians, but he was involved in one conflict that took some creative effort to resolve. He believed the White Sox owed him $200 for a matter not covered by his contract. I explained his argument to their management, but their version of the facts was different, and they refused to pay. We went back and forth a few times, with both sides restating their position, but no payment was forthcoming.

Warren Hacker called his time with the Indians "maybe the best days I ever had in baseball."

I sided with Warren's position and wanted to get away from my role as the middle man in their dispute. So, I approached Ownie Bush with a solution. We had slightly more than $200 in the office vault from "late gate" receipts—money collected from fans who arrived at games after the ticket booths had closed and paid a ticket-taker at the front gate to enter the stadium. That money was then turned over at the end of the evening.

Ownie agreed with me that Warren had delivered more than $200 in value to the Indians and it made sense to pay him out of what essentially was petty cash. It wasn't a huge amount of money, although in the early 1960s it amounted to more than a week's salary for most people. It was typical of the kind of issue that comes up in baseball that often goes unresolved and leaves players with negative feelings toward their teams.

Warren went on to pitch four more seasons for Indianapolis, performing well as a relief pitcher until retiring in 1966 at age 41.

The most interesting player on the 1962 team, though, might have been pitcher Herb Score, who, like Simpson and Hacker, was trying to revive his career.

Score had broken into professional baseball in Indianapolis in 1952 at 19 years old, and played for the Indians again in 1954. He went 22 – 5 that season to propel himself into the Majors. He then won American League Rookie of the Year honors with Cleveland in '55 after leading the league in strikeouts and repeated that feat the following season while winning 20 games. He was an All-Star selection each of his first two seasons in the Majors and appeared headed for a great career.

A series of injuries kept Score from achieving that level of success again, however, most notably being hit above the eye by a line drive in 1957. He returned to the Indians after appearing in four games for the White Sox early in the '62 season. He was only 29 years old, but the injuries had taken their toll and he was trying to revive his career. He went 10 – 7 for the Indians with a 4.82 ERA. He also produced a highlight in the All-Star game played in Indianapolis. As the first-place team, the Indians hosted the game and faced a collection of All-Stars from the other five league teams. Score was the winning pitcher and went two-for-two at the plate.

We also had a pitcher that season named Franklin Kreutzer, a left-hander who finished with a 15 – 10 record and a 3.29 earned run average. He had defeated Louisville in every game in which he faced them during the regular season, so he figured to be a great asset heading into our playoff series against the Colonels. Appling, though, didn't list him as a starter for any of the games. I asked Luke why, and he said, "They'll bunt him out of the ballpark." That didn't make sense to me, because it hadn't happened during the regular season. But Appling insisted, and Louisville swept us, 3 – 0, in the series.

Luke was voted Manager of the Year, just as Cot Deal had been the previous season, but I'll never understand his decision regarding Kreutzer. Appling, however, soon became the victim of another surprising decision.

Although he performed well as our manager during the regular season, he didn't win over Mr. Bush. Ownie wanted the manager to come by his office the morning after home games to discuss whatever had happened the previous night and to provide a status report on the team. Most managers didn't like to do it—understandably, because they had been up late the previous night. Cot Deal did it often enough to appease Ownie, but Appling seldom did it. Ownie didn't like him because of that, despite the team's success.

Luke saw the writing on the wall because of that issue and caught on as a major-league coach with the Baltimore Orioles after the season. His only chance to manage in the Majors came over the final 40 games of the 1967 season, when he replaced Alvin Dark with the Kansas City Athletics.

His experience reminded me of mine working for Mr. Cardarelli in the drug store. You might not like the boss but he's always the boss, and you challenge him at your own risk. ●

DENNY MCLAIN

Denny McLain was a promising pitcher in the Chicago White Sox farm system in the early 1960s while we were their Triple-A affiliate. They let McLain get away. McLain was battling for a roster spot with another pitcher, Bruce Howard, in spring training before the 1963 season. Under the rules of that time, players with one year of service in the minor leagues were subject to a draft if they had not been promoted to the major-league team, aside from one protected player. To help reach a decision who to promote and who to leave unprotected, White Sox executives had McLain and Howard pitch against each other in a spring-training game.

It might sound strange today, knowing that McLain won a record 31 games for Detroit in 1968, but in 1963 nobody could be certain of his future. He had compiled a combined 5 – 8 record for two White Sox Class D teams with a 2.97 earned run average in the 1962 season, while Howard had gone 7 – 3 with a 2.34 ERA at the Class D level.

Their pitch-off drew a huge crowd of front office personnel, myself included. I have no opinion on who pitched better that day—it seemed pretty much a standoff to me—but the White Sox liked Howard's personality better and considered him a better fit for their organization. McLain went unprotected despite being a native of Chicago. The White Sox still wanted to keep him in the organization, but he failed to clear waivers. Had he gone unclaimed, he likely would have pitched for the Indians at some point on his way to the Majors. But Detroit claimed

Denny McLain, shown with Bob Hope and Bob Gibson, was on top of the baseball world in 1968. Tougher times were ahead, however.

him and the rest is history. A lot of history.

McLain pitched for Detroit's Triple-A affiliate in Syracuse in 1964, then reached the Majors the following season. He had three consecutive standout seasons before peaking with 31 victories in 1968, becoming the first pitcher to reach the 30-win plateau since Dizzy Dean in 1934, and still the most recent to do it. His ERA was just 1.96 that season and he threw 28 complete games.

He won 24 games the following season and repeated as the Cy Young Award winner, but his career and life collapsed after that. He was suspended for gambling and carrying a gun on a team flight among other violations and served two prison sentences for drug trafficking, embezzlement, racketeering, mail fraud, and conspiracy.

McLain eventually wound up pitching in Bush Stadium, but against the Indians instead of for them. Playing for Iowa in 1973 during a comeback attempt that ultimately failed, he was shelled for 12 hits and five earned runs in 4 2/3 innings in the second half of a doubleheader on June 6. His fame was such that he drew the largest crowd of the season to that point—2,102.

McLain's weight ballooned past 300 pounds following his playing career, partly due to his Pepsi addiction. He often drank a case a day during his playing career, and continued to do so after he was forced out of baseball. He even drank a case of Pepsi while broadcasting a game for Iowa when they played the Indians at Bush Stadium in the late 1980s, when he was both the franchise's general manager and broadcast analyst.

Howard's career was far less eventful. He pitched in the Majors from 1963 – 68, compiling a 26 – 31 record. He played for the Indians in 1964, going 15 – 8 with a league-best ERA of 2.20, and again in 1967 when he went 3 – 0 with a .327 ERA.

We can only wonder how history would have been rewritten if the White Sox had protected McLain instead of Howard. It no doubt would have made life more interesting in Indianapolis, though. ●

1963

I ndianapolis Indians manager Luke Appling wasn't the only one facing termination following the 1962 season. The entire American Association was nearing an end. It had been barely hanging on with just six teams the previous two years, and when Omaha dropped out, the league had no choice but to fold. ● The Indians then joined the much healthier International League, which consisted of 10 teams divided into Southern and Northern divisions. Rollie Hemsley, who had played 19 seasons as a journeyman catcher in the Majors, including a rookie season in Pittsburgh when Ownie Bush managed the Pirates, became our next manager.

Rollie's nickname was Rollickin' Rollie because he had been a heavy drinker during his playing career, so much so that he was let go by four teams. He overcame the problem by joining Alcoholics Anonymous. He revealed his membership in that group in 1940, becoming the first nationally known person to do so and setting an example for others to confront their problem. He was still a nondrinker when he managed the Indians, and my experience with him was terrific. I had several meals with him and never saw him drink anything other than

The 1963 team, led by manager Rollie Hemsley, won a third consecutive pennant for the Indianapolis Indians.

endless cups of coffee.

He was a good manager, too. He had proved that in 1950 when he was named the Minor League Manager of the Year by *The Sporting News* after directing the Double-A Columbus Red Birds. He proved it again as he led us to an 86 – 67 record.

It was a dramatic season on several counts. We started slowly, trailing Atlanta by seven games in the third week of June, but stormed back to take an eight-game lead in the Southern Division on July 14 after winning 14 of 19 games. After later falling 3 1/2 games behind Atlanta, we forced a tie for the division title. We won a coin flip to host a one-game playoff and won that game, 1 – 0, on Fritz Ackley's two-hit, six-strikeout, one-walk pitching gem. Charlie Smith, our shortstop, drove in the winning run with a bloop single to left with two outs in the fourth inning after Lou Vassie led off the inning with a walk and reached third on Koranda's single.

We then won a third consecutive pennant by defeating Northern Division winner Syracuse in five games. Joe Shipley, who had gone 15 – 7 in the regular season, won two of the games. And this time we didn't flame out in the championship series, defeating Atlanta—which

Herb Score's last baseball stop was with the Indianapolis Indians after injuries derailed a standout major league career.

had finished one game behind us in the division—in five games in the Governor's Cup finals.

Don Buford turned in one of the greatest seasons of any Indianapolis Indians player, hitting .336 in the regular season and then .450 in the playoffs. He led the International League in batting average, runs (114), hits, (206), doubles (41), and stolen bases (42) and was voted both the league's Most Valuable Player and Rookie of the Year. Ackley, who was the ERA champion and finished 18 – 5, was honored as the Pitcher of the Year.

Hemsley was named by *The Sporting News* as its Minor League Manager of the Year, making him our third different manager to receive the award in three consecutive seasons.

Just as with Appling the previous year, I had a conflict with him in the playoffs.

Rollie was feeling good about our chances to win the title after we took a 2 – 1 lead at home. The day before we were to fly to Atlanta to resume the series, he told me he had given Herb Score permission to skip the trip. Score had not been a factor in the '63 season, going 0 – 6 with a 7.66 ERA, and Rollie didn't think he would be needed in the final games.

I protested, saying it wasn't fair to the rest of the guys that one player be excused. Rollie told me I would have to talk with Score because he had already given him permission to go home. Herb didn't like to fly, and often took a train to the road games. I approved of that privilege extended to him as a major-league veteran, but thought it was important for him to stay with the team for the final playoff games.

Herb agreed to join the team in Atlanta, and most likely traveled by train to get there. We won the series there and Herb probably went on from there to his offseason home in Florida. I never heard from him again, and that was the end of his baseball career. He was just 30 years old, a great career ended too soon by injuries.

That season also was notable for the late-season activation of 42-year-old coach Ted Beard. He had broken into professional baseball as a 21-year-old in Pittsburgh's minor-league organization in 1942. After serving in World War II, he played seven major-league seasons, but also appeared in 13 consecutive seasons for the Indians. He went hitless in four at-bats over two games to conclude his playing career after rosters were expanded.

Some players regarded Beard as the club's "real" manager late in the season. Regardless, Hemsley suffered a fate similar to that of Luke Appling the previous year. Rollie asked me if Ownie Bush intended to bring him back the following season. I already knew Ownie wasn't planning to do so, but I thought he should be the one to tell Rollie.

I was headed for New York, where the Yankees were hosting World Series games against the Dodgers, and told Mr. Bush I would be staying in the same hotel as Rollie. He told me to have Rollie call him at a specific time on a specific day.

A day or two after that scheduled time, I saw Rollie in the hotel, and he told me Ownie hadn't taken his call. I apologized to Rollie and told him Ownie didn't plan to bring him back. He deserved to know as soon as possible because he was around so many other baseball executives during the Series games in New York and needed the opportunity to look for another job.

Rollie managed Cincinnati's Single-A team in Cedar Rapids, Iowa the following season, but didn't manage again until he came back to lead Kansas City's Single-A team in Waterloo, Iowa in 1969. That was the end of his baseball career.

Lou Vassie provided one of my lasting memories of the 1963 season.

We had assumed his contract from the Phillies before the 1962 season, at $800 per month. He had been a valuable member of the team that won the American Association pennant in 1962. Before the 1963 season, however, White Sox farm director Glenn Miller mailed a contract to me for Vassie to sign for the same amount he had been paid in '62. I called Glenn and suggested Lou get a raise because he had played so well for us. Miller said, "No, no, that's enough, he's just a Triple-A utility infielder."

So, I sent the contract to Lou at his home in Louisville. He didn't respond for a while, which made me wonder what he was thinking, but he eventually mailed the signed contract back with no comment.

He had an even better season in 1963, batting .280 and playing outstanding defense again. But in January of '64, the White Sox sent another contract for him for the upcoming season at the same salary.

I called Glenn Miller again and said, "Glenn, we talked about this last year. This guy's a good player. He had a good season again for a championship team and now for the third year in a row you want him to work for the same amount of money?"

"He's a utility infielder," Glenn said. "That's all we're going to pay him."

So, I dutifully forwarded the contract to Vassie in January, same as the year before. He hung onto it for a month or so and then mailed it back unsigned with a courteous letter saying he had decided to retire from baseball. He added that he had a civilian job lined up with an oil company. He was just 27 years old and had been playing in the minors for nine seasons, so the lack of confidence from the White Sox led him to decide it was time to give up on a major-league career.

I sent the White Sox a copy of his letter and followed up with a phone call, hoping they would offer him a better contract. They didn't care. Their thinking was that utility infielders were easy to find for minor-league teams.

But then we go to spring training in 1964 and suddenly the White Sox find themselves short of infielders with about a week left before the start of the season. Glenn Miller called me into his office at the training site and told me to call Vassie to ask him to report to Sarasota for the final days of spring training.

I said, "Glenn, I've been telling you for two years we should pay him more and you wouldn't do it! If you want him in Chicago, you call him; I'm not calling him."

Glenn called Lou and the White Sox flew him to Chicago. He worked out for them for a day or two and they offered him a major-league contract for the season—at the minimum salary. He said no thanks and went back to Louisville. He probably would have been paid $7,000 or $8,000 on a major-league minimum deal, much more than what he would have earned in a minor-league season, but he was tired of being nickel-and-dimed.

I've told that story to some of our players over the years and they can't believe anyone would walk away from a major-league contract after working so long to get one. But I've always admired Lou tremendously for taking a stand for himself and fair treatment.

That story tells you how baseball management would jerk guys around in that era. It held all the power over minor leaguers and would tell them to take or leave whatever it offered them. We should have taken better care of Lou. If we had done the right thing, the logical thing, the White Sox would have had access to his services in 1964 when they needed him.

I was caught in the middle of it and just did what I was told, but I felt bad for him. They easily could have paid him another $50 a month or so while with the Indians—just something to show a little appreciation. That seemed ridiculous to me. Again, it reminded me of my experience in the drug store with Mr. Cardarelli, when I wanted another nickel an hour. Sometimes management can be penny wise and pound foolish. It wouldn't have taken much of an investment to keep me in the drug store, or to keep Lou in baseball.

He never complained to me about the situation, but I know he would have stayed in baseball if he had been treated more fairly. He just loved to put on the uniform and play the game. We remained friends, though. He contributed to baseball in various capacities after retiring, such as volunteering as a coach at a high school in Louisville. He came up to Indianapolis with his wife to see a game each season for many years, and when we moved to our new downtown ballpark, I talked him into donating his Indians jersey. We framed it and hung it in one of the suites.

The White Sox did all right without him in 1964, going 98 – 64 and finishing one game behind the Yankees in the American League pennant race. Maybe Lou Vassie could have helped them win one more game. We'll never know. ●

Vassie's donated jersey and gear were hung in a suite honoring him.

Les Moss, who managed the Indianapolis Indians in 1964 and '66, proved to be a formidable arm-wrestling opponent.

MY CONFESSION

I think it's safe to reveal something. Something that happened on an airplane. Something involving alcohol that was kept under wraps. Until now. The Indians won the American Association regular-season championship in 1961 and '62, the International League title in 1963, and finished one game back of the Pacific Coast League Eastern Division leader in 1964.

The 1965 team slipped to a losing season, but we hit stride again in 1966 when we contended for the Pacific Coast league Eastern Division title. We were hanging on to a tie for first place with Tulsa early in August, but then hit a terrible slump. After we were swept in a four-game series in Denver that ended on August 25, we were 3 1/2 games back of the division lead and had lost 20 of our previous 24 games.

We were running out of time, so I came up with what I thought was a great idea to give the team a spark. I called our manager, Les Moss, after the final game in Denver and said, "Why don't you buy some booze and loosen up this team?"

He couldn't believe it, but I told him I was serious. We always permitted beer on our chartered flights, but I thought the team was playing tight and everyone needed to have some fun for one day. So I told Les to go out and buy some hard liquor for the flight to Tulsa.

It didn't work. We lost three of four games in Tulsa and then came back to Indianapolis and lost the first three games of that series to drop out of the race. It didn't help that we lost our right fielder, Bill Voss, to a broken finger before the series in Tulsa.

What was reported to the newspapers was that Voss had broken the middle finger on his right hand during a rundown in the final game in Denver. According to the *Indianapolis News,* "Voss was injured in a collision with Marty Martinez while running the bases."

What was actually true was that Voss had broken his finger arm-wrestling with Moss on the flight to Tulsa. Apparently the alcohol emboldened Voss, who stood 6-foot-2 and weighed all of 160 pounds, and he challenged Moss, who had served as a Merchant Marine in World War II and then played 13 seasons as a 205-pound catcher.

Moss-Voss was not a fair fight. Les put Bill down so quickly and so violently that Voss suffered the broken finger. He had indeed been in a rundown between second and third base in the sixth inning of the last game in Denver because of a baserunning error, so that provided an explanation for the injury. That certainly sounded better to the public than a drunken arm wrestling contest on an airplane.

Voss was lost for the rest of the season, which didn't help the Indians' cause. He was a player with some major-league experience, was hitting .252 at the time of his injury, and was an outstanding fielder. He went on to play six more major-league seasons for the White Sox, Angels, Brewers, Athletics, and Cardinals.

I learned the truth after the team returned to Indianapolis when Moss came into my office, closed the door and said, "You know how you told me to put liquor on the airplane?"

I thought he was reminding me to repay him for the alcohol, so I said, "Just give me the receipt."

He went on to explain how Voss had challenged him to the arm wrestling contest, and how easily he had won. "And you know how damn weak he is!" Moss added.

We kept the truth from the media and the White Sox, but 15 or 20 years later, I finally confessed to C. V. Davis, the White Sox farm director, when he stopped by my office on his way to Florida for spring training.

He thanked me for telling him and said, "I never did believe that story. I always wondered what happened."

I'm not proud of what I did, but I was a competitive guy and was aggressive about trying to win championships. The team was playing uptight, and I thought a good party would help it relax.

It didn't work, obviously. The Indians finished 70 – 78 that season. I guess the moral of the story is that drinking and deception do not pay off. ●

Max helped rejuvenate Bill Fischer's baseball career in 1965 by convincing him to report to spring training.

BILL FISCHER

B ill Fischer had a long career in baseball, as a pitcher, pitching coach, and minor-league instructor and administrator. He entered professional baseball in 1948 at the age of 17 for the Class-D affiliate of the White Sox. He worked as the "senior pitching adviser" for the Kansas City Royals up to his death, at 87, in October of 2018. ⬤ I played a role in keeping his career alive in 1965.

Bill had pitched continuously in the Majors from 1956 – 64, except for a brief return to Triple A early in the 1962 season. He set a major-league record that still stands by working 84 1/3 consecutive innings without allowing a walk.

His '64 season with the Minnesota Twins did not go well. He suffered an ankle injury, and stopped pitching on June 1 with an 0 – 1 record and 7.4 ERA in nine appearances. He spent the rest of the season as a scout and minor-league pitching instructor for the Twins, but was released over the winter.

The White Sox, for whom he had pitched in the 1950s, invited him to spring training as a nonroster player. He anticipated a situation where he would just be used to throw batting practice and not be given a legitimate chance to make their roster, so he planned to retire from playing.

I wanted him to pitch for Indianapolis, though, and, as a friend, I wanted to keep him in baseball so he could maintain a positive relationship with Major League Baseball and prepare for a coaching career. I called him and was able to persuade him to come to spring training once again, at the age of 34.

He didn't make the White Sox roster, but he enjoyed one of the highlights of his career for us that season. He was a relief pitcher, but on May 3 manager George Noga asked him to make a start—his first since 1963—to give our starters an extra day's rest. Bill responded by showing the control that was the hallmark of his career, throwing a complete-game victory over San Diego by allowing just five hits and no walks. He threw just 90 pitches, 70 of them strikes, in a game that lasted just 1 hour and 38 minutes.

Afterward, he called the victory "one of my greatest baseball thrills."

He never did get called up by the White Sox, but wound up pitching four seasons for the Indians and went 42 – 29. He loved Indianapolis, and spent much of his free time walking around downtown to explore the war monuments. He continued to do that when he returned to the city as a coach with visiting teams.

He was the pitching coach for Cincinnati from 1979 – 83, then for Boston from 1985 – 91. He was back in Triple A with Richmond after the Red Sox let him go, but got an offer to return to the Majors from the Tampa Bay Rays in 1999. He happened to be in Indianapolis when the call came, and I arranged his flight to Florida.

It had been 35 years since I convinced him to keep pitching, and it was great to contribute to his career once again.

PROMOTIONS

S ome fans are happy just to come out and see a baseball game, but others need an added incentive to come out to the ballpark. That's why minor-league general managers are obligated to find unique ways to promote their teams. I learned that early on, and have witnessed some innovative attempts to improve attendance. I've tried a few myself in an attempt to keep black ink from turning red. My second season with the Indians in 1958, I convinced Dr. Al G. Wright, the director of the Purdue All-American Marching Band, to bring his group to a game. They were supposed to march on the field before a Sunday afternoon game, but a previous rainout forced us to play a doubleheader that day so they marched between games. Their Golden Girl baton twirler performed as well.

Walker Cooper was the player-manager that season. He had concluded his major-league career the previous season with the St. Louis Cardinals, with whom he had begun his career in 1940. He was 43 years old when he came to the Indians, and hoping to get back to the Majors as a manager. It certainly wasn't going to happen as a player. He caught 18 games and pinch-hit in 20 others for the Indians that season, but batted only .211.

He was part of one memorable play as a catcher, though. Someone hit a foul ball that went straight up and nearly hit him on the head coming down. He never moved, unaware of where the ball had been hit, and it landed right next to him.

He made another memorable contribution via a promotion at the end of that season. The Indians had lost $60,000 in 1957 and were headed toward another major loss, so we were desperate to do anything that would draw a few more fans to a game. Before the final home game of the season on September 1, we conducted our annual three-inning exhibition between the local newspaper and broadcast personalities. Cooper's daughter, 19-year-old Sara Ann, provided an additional attraction by dancing the Charleston on our dugout roof between innings. She had been selected Miss Missouri and won the talent competition in the Miss America contest in 1957, so it was nothing new to her. She "acquitted herself well" according to a newspaper account.

It would have been more appropriate if the game had been played against Charleston, which won the American Association pennant that season, but Wichita was the opponent. The Indians lost the game to finish 72 – 82, but drew a better-than-average crowd of 3,015 that night.

○

Some of our best promotions involved Hall of Fame pitcher Bob Feller during the 1960s. He was a real pro, and great to work with.

His fee initially was about $300. That was a good payday for him because he knew how to keep his expenses at a minimum, and, in turn, kept ours low as well. He was a licensed pilot and flew himself to Indianapolis, and he had an endorsement deal with a hotel chain that covered his lodging. He'd always give us an honest day's work. He'd fly in the night before the game, give a talk at a luncheon the day of the game and grant interviews to the media as well. He pitched to local celebrities before the game and tried to make it easy for them to hit the ball hard so they could say they got a hit off Bob Feller. He then roamed the stands during the game to sign autographs.

I never dickered with him, because I knew what other teams were paying him. After his first appearance, he called back every year for about five years and asked to come back. I said, "Sure, you did a great job for us last year. We'd love to have you come back."

When I asked about the fee, he'd give a slightly higher price than the previous year. That was fine; I was happy with him and wasn't going to negotiate over minor increases.

Now fast-forward many years. My nephew, Gary Turner, lived in Las Vegas and went to an appearance Feller was making there. He told Feller I was his uncle, and asked Feller if he remembered me. Feller said, "Sure, he's the tightest man in America!"

I couldn't believe he said that, but found it amusing. I always gave him what he wanted. How could he complain about that?

One night, Feller was in town when the Massey Ferguson Co. rented out the ballpark. They had become bored with their annual event, so I suggested they bring in Feller. He was a farm boy from Iowa, so he seemed to be an appropriate entertainer for a company that manufactured tractors. I gave them Feller's phone number, and they made a deal to bring him in by giving him a tractor in exchange for his services.

Many years later, I was reading a story about Feller and he was talking about all the equipment he had in his barn in Ohio. He mentioned having three tractors. I know one of them had to have come from Massey Ferguson.

○

Not all the performers you bring in work out the way you hope, however. One of those was Max Patkin. He was a former minor-league pitcher and World War II veteran who developed an act to entertain fans at games. He was a scrawny man with a rubber face who accentuated his comedic appearance by wearing a dirty, baggy uniform with a question mark on the back instead of a number, wore his cap sideways and made faces while clowning during games. He made his living barnstorming the United States and Canada, performing mostly at minor-league games.

He appeared in Indianapolis a few times in the 1960s. Ownie Bush wasn't a fan and didn't want him to work our games, but Max came to me nearly in tears about not getting a chance to continue working in Indianapolis. I was honest with him, telling him Mr. Bush didn't like his act, but said we would revisit the possibility at some point. I kept my word to him. After I became the general manager, I booked him.

I have to admit, I didn't like his act either. He would begin the game by coaching first base. He rolled around in the dirt and just generally tried to be funny, such as by putting water in his mouth, laying on his back and spitting it up into the air like a whale. If you've seen it once . . .

Our most profitable promotion generally came on the "buyout nights," when a company or organization would rent out the ballpark and distribute tickets to customers and/or employees. The United Auto Workers was one of our regular clients for those special games, and they wanted Max to entertain. They always brought a big crowd because they gave away so many tickets, but Max later claimed to have been the reason 14,000 fans were on hand when he performed for the Indians. The truth is, they would have been there anyway.

In later years, The Famous Chicken had a similar act, only better, and he actually could draw a huge crowd. He performed at Indians games for 35 years beginning in 1981. In his first appearance for us, when he was known as the San Diego Chicken, he drew 12,218 fans for a Friday night game in July in the midst of a losing season. We had drawn 1,149 fans the previous night.

The Chicken, whose real name is Ted Giannoulas, is probably the most beloved mascot in the history of sports, and inspired the creation of mascots around the world. He was a natural promoter, always going the extra mile. Our broadcaster, Howard Kellman, would occasionally run into him at a road game when he was working for another team and record a promotional announcement with him to be aired on the radio. He would say something like, "I'm going to be in Indianapolis on [date] and I guarantee the fowlest night of the year!"

He wasn't always the easiest guy to work with, though. I didn't like the fact he got little kids to put on chicken costumes and follow him around and raise their leg as they walked past the umpire, like a dog walking past a fire hydrant. I once suggested he not do that, but I didn't order him to stop, and he didn't.

○

The most consistently profitable venture for us was our annual exhibition game against the Big Red Machine teams of Cincinnati in the 1970s. It usually drew a sellout crowd, or close to it, and the revenue from that one game might mean the difference between a profitable season or not. Our play-by-play broadcaster, Howard Kellman, says that, when he joined the Indians in 1974, manager Vern Rapp told him the only time he would see me nervous was if it rained the day of the exhibition game against the Reds.

Sure enough, on June 20 of that year, the day the Reds were coming to town, the skies were overcast and rain fell throughout the afternoon. Only a mist was falling as the game began, however, and while a hard rain poured down merely five blocks away, we were able to play the game. The lead paragraph in the next day's Star described the backdrop to the game as "great lightning flashes and the roar of thunder," but we played the game in relative comfort before a crowd of 10,161 fans.

I'm told I said afterward, "This makes up for all the bad luck I've ever had in my life."

The fans got a good show that night, too. Johnny Bench hit a two-run homer in the third inning, but the Indians won, 7 – 5. After the game, Indians catcher Sonny Ruberto admitted to Howard he tipped off Bench that a fastball was coming. Our pitcher, Pat Zachry, wasn't in on the conspiracy, but it all worked out for the best. The fans got what they came to see. They would cheer for the Reds until the backups came into the game, and then they would switch to the Indians.

The ideal scenario was for the Reds star players to get hits and for the Indians to win.

The problem was that most of those star players left the game after batting in the top of the first inning, took a shower and headed back to Cincinnati. They often wouldn't even play in the field. That was understandable, because the exhibitions meant nothing to them and they didn't want to risk injury, but it made me think we weren't playing square with the fans.

○

One of our better promotions—for a while—was offered in the early 1990s. We originally called it Used Car Night, but changed that to Win a Car Night. We made arrangements with 10 local auto dealers to bring over one car each with a value of $3,000. We gave them tickets to distribute to customers in return. Howard Kellman, our play-by-play broadcaster and ace salesman, made it happen by pounding the pavement and working out the details.

We conducted a drawing between innings and each winner was given his or her car and title on the spot. The idea was to offer fans a dependable second car, or a car for a high school or college student.

It went well for a few years, but eventually some of the dealers began bringing over cars that weren't worth the agreed-upon value. They tried to use the occasion to get rid of some of the junkers on their lot. We had some of our grounds crew members test drive the cars to assess their worth, because they were driving similar cars themselves and knew better than anyone else. If a car didn't appear to be worth $3,000, we'd call the offending dealer to request a better car and wind up in a debate over Blue Book values.

One year we had two winners for the same car. One of the numbers drawn did not produce a winner, so another ticket was drawn. Shortly after, the holder of the ticket with the first number emerged from the rest room to claim his car. We wound up giving the car to one of the fans and check for $3,000 to the other. From then on, we announced that if a ticket wasn't claimed in time, it was void.

○

Fireworks have been our longest-running and most dependable promotion for drawing fans. Early on in my time with the Indians, we didn't shoot off fireworks after a game on July 4 because the local Sahara Grotto had a popular display at Butler University's football stadium, and we didn't want to compete with that. We normally would have ours a day earlier.

The only real problem I recall was the year at Bush Stadium when the local company with whom we had contracted brought out the fireworks during the afternoon and placed them under a tarp beyond the wire fence that ran across the deepest part of center field. The grass was wet, however, and some of the fireworks were ruined.

I called the owner, Bob Casse, to tell him we needed replacements. He said he didn't know if they had anything left in their warehouse.

"Bob, this is why I hired you in the first place," I said. "You're a local businessman; you have a warehouse here in Indianapolis. You need to find more and get them out to Bush Stadium immediately, if not sooner."

He said he would check again, and sure enough his sons came out with replacement fireworks while the game was going on. We opened the left field gate to let in their truck, and the night was saved.

We make it a point to have our show on July 4, because it leads up to the city's major fireworks show, which is shot from the top of one of downtown Indianapolis's tallest buildings. Our fans can watch our display and then stay in their seats for a good view of the show thousands of people drive downtown to watch from city streets.

Instead of avoiding the city's major fireworks display as we once did, we're able to capitalize on it. The International League assists by always allowing us to have a home game on July 4. Some teams don't want a home game on that date because they don't want to compete with their city's show, but it's a guaranteed sellout and a very profitable evening for the Indians. We also shoot off fireworks after Friday night home games during the season.

○

One of our more memorable promotions involved Indiana University basketball coach Bob Knight. It wasn't to benefit the Indians, however. It was to raise money for Landon Turner, a starting forward on the 1981 NCAA championship team Knight had coached. Turner was paralyzed in an automobile accident while driving to Kings Island in Cincinnati in July of 1981, and various efforts were made to help with his medical expenses.

The Fourth of July fireworks show is always one of the most successful promotions.

One of our staff members, Kurt Hunt, suggested we join the cause. So, before a game at Bush Stadium on August 26 that summer, we had Landon Turner Night. Some of Knight's former Indiana players took part in a home run hitting contest against his pitching. None of them managed a home run, but none of the 5,400-plus fans in attendance cared. The Indians were able to donate $34,358.91 to the Turner Trust Fund.

My predominant memory of the evening is from walking Knight down to the field before the game. As we passed my general manager's office, he saw Star sportswriter Max Stultz and walked over and slugged him in the arm—hard! For Knight, however, that was a show of affection. Stultz just smiled and said hello. As we continued on our way, Knight said some people had told him to watch out for Stultz when he first arrived at Indiana, but he had found Stultz to be fair and professional.

I saw Max a couple of hours later in the press box and asked how his arm was feeling. Max said he was fine, that the punch was "nothing, really." I said, "Nothing?! He really popped you." But Max said Knight hadn't used his knuckles when he punched, just the flat part of his fist.

○

We also have rented out our park when the Indians are out of town to assist our bottom line.

Professional wrestling always provided profitable entertainment for us back in the days of Victory Field/Bush Stadium. The wrestlers came in three or four times a season and we received 15 percent of the total gate and 100 percent of the concessions. We set up a ring over home plate and placed chairs around it, while other fans sat in the grandstand.

Dick the Bruiser and Wilbur Snyder ran the wrestling operation in central Indiana, and they were great to work with. They're legendary in the wrestling world, especially Bruiser, whose birth name was William

Afflis, but went by Richard Afflis. I dealt primarily with Snyder, who handled most of the business side of the operation.

I never let them use the Indians clubhouse for the matches because a lot of the players kept their street clothes and equipment there while the team was on the road. They had to use the visitor's clubhouse on the first base side. It was funny to see, because they would create all this mayhem in the ring during the matches, making it look like World War III might break out as they went at one another, and then I'd see them in the locker room joking around together afterward. Some of the fans would have been surprised to see that.

They also might have been surprised to hear what Bruiser said one night when I was walking toward the parking lot at the end of the evening with Snyder and him. Bruiser suddenly stopped and said, "Oh, I forgot that damn trophy!" That helps you put wrestling in perspective. In most sports a world championship trophy is a big deal. But in wrestling those trophies get passed around routinely, according to the script. They have a world's championship match nearly every week, so the trophy is easy to forget when you're heading home after a match.

The only mishap we had with the wrestlers involved Indians employee Wes Gilbert, an electrician. He sat at ringside for the matches and tended to any electric problems that came up. He also held the microphone for the ring announcer. Most nights, all he had to do was turn on the microphone and hand it to the announcer and then take it back. But one night, some numbskull who was unhappy with the way the match was going, or just wanted to hit the wrestler he didn't like, threw a heavy rock. It fell short of the ring and hit Wes in the back of the head. We had to take him to the hospital to get him stitched up.

I never had to worry about mishaps on the business side of the matches, though. The day after the event, I mailed a bill to Snyder for the ballpark rental and the money due the ushers and security personnel. He always sent a check back by return mail the next day. They always paid on time and gave what I considered an accurate count of the advance ticket sales.

○

We didn't have as much luck with rock shows at the stadium. Particularly one in the 1970s.

Groundskeeper Ike Ives convinced me to place the stage against the wire home run fence in centerfield and let the audience sit on the grass in the outfield, rather than putting it over home plate and making everyone sit in the stands as we did for the wrestling shows. That turned out to be a big mistake. It rained, so all those young adults who were supposed to be sitting in the outfield were running all over the place and sliding in the grass. One guy was body-surfing on the pitching mound. They built some fires in the outfield, too, because it got cold after it rained.

When I went out to inspect the damage the following day, I could smell something I had never experienced before. It was marijuana. I had been in college, in the Army, and around a lot of people in baseball, but I had never smelled marijuana to that point in my life.

We had damages in both the outfield and the infield. I called our manager at the time, Vern Rapp, while the team was on the road and didn't sugarcoat anything. There was one particularly damaged area near first base. The team was coming home in a few days and there was no way to get everything back in good condition again. I was pretty shook up about it, but he said, "It'll be fine. Don't worry about it."

We kept our field at Bush Stadium in great shape. The stadium might have been falling apart brick by brick, but we took great pride in the playing field. It turned out OK when we played the next game. I didn't hear any players complain about it, and neither did Vern.

Given that experience, I wasn't too keen on having another rock concert at the ballpark. But the following year some governing body in Evansville had banned a concert, so the promoters came to me in desperation. I told them I didn't want to do it. I said, "I'd like to have the money, but you don't have enough money to rent the park." I just didn't want to go through it again.

They came back to me again in an even greater state of anxiety, so

I threw a deal at them I thought they would refuse. I also told them the city would have to approve it as well. They agreed to it and gave me a deposit.

I called Bill Spencer, who was the head of the parks and recreation at the time, in the administration of Mayor Richard Lugar. He talked to Lugar and came back and said the city wanted an extra $10,000 for itself. I might be a little off on those numbers, but that seems right to me.

I called one of the promoters and told him about the city's demand. He wasn't happy about it, but said he would talk to his partner. When I arrived at work the next day, he was waiting for me to sign a contract. He came up to my office and counted out $100 bills until he got to $10,000. We needed more money from the ticket agency, Ross and Babcock, and, once we got that, we wrote a check to the city for their share.

That show turned out great. We had learned from our mistakes of the previous year. We had more security, we roped off the infield and we wrote it into the contract that nobody could set foot in that area. The fans sat in the outfield and were orderly during the concert.

I stood with a friend from a spot near one of the entrances to the grandstand seating area during the concert. At one point a little dog got loose and ran onto the infield grass. One of the security people ducked under the rope and went to get the dog.

"When you say nobody gets on the infield, you really mean it, don't you?" my friend said. ◉

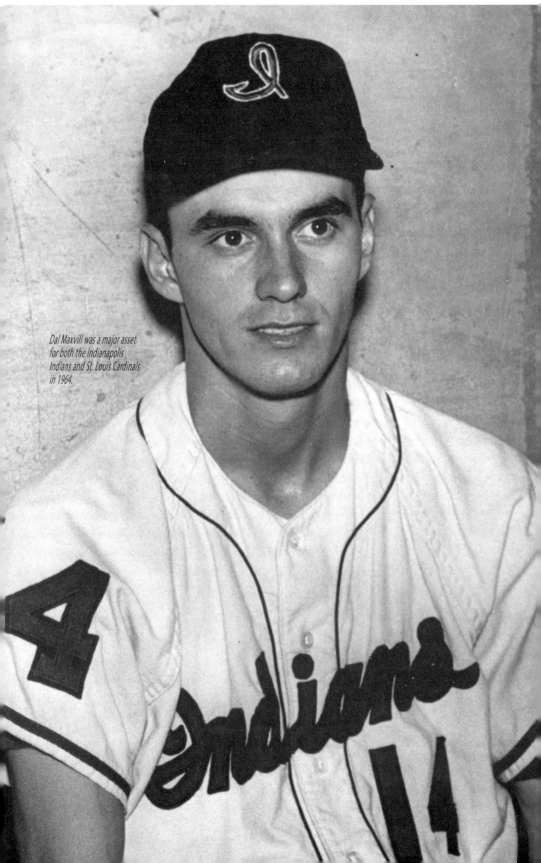

Dal Maxvill was a major asset for both the Indianapolis Indians and St. Louis Cardinals in 1964.

DAL MAXVILL

T he Indianapolis Indians' streak of pennant-winning seasons ended in 1964, but the season was no
less dramatic than the three previous to it. ● We were
dropped from the International League because the major-league clubs refused to renew the travel subsidy that
had been paid to the eight International League franchises in 1963. Our only option was to join the Pacific Coast League (along with Arkansas) and become the
eastern-most member of the 12-team circuit.

We also had a new manager, Les Moss, but many of the players
from the previous season returned. We won 89 games, more than in
'61 and '63 and matching the total of the '62 team, but finished seven
games behind Arkansas in the Eastern Division. To give you an idea
how far west the league stretched, teams from Denver, Dallas, and Salt
Lake City were in the Eastern Division. The Western Division included
teams in Hawaii, California, Oregon, and Washington.

We were 4,391 miles from Hawaii, but Major League Baseball
agreed to reimburse Arkansas and the Indianapolis Indians for travel
expenses beyond what we had spent the previous year.

We started the 1964 season slowly, owning a 22 – 34 record in
June, but got a spark from shortstop Dal Maxvill. I had seen Dal in

spring training while he was playing for the St. Louis Triple-A affiliate in Jacksonville. He caught your eye because he was so fluid, and he already had played 132 games for St. Louis over the previous two seasons.

We needed a shortstop, so I called the Cardinals' farm director Eddie Stanky to see if he would option Maxvill to us. They didn't seem to need him very badly; he was riding the bench in Jacksonville behind a guy named Cooter Veal.

Stanky kept talking as if he planned to send Maxvill to us, but wouldn't pull the trigger. After a couple of weeks, I called White Sox general manager Eddie Short and told him I couldn't get Stanky to make the move. He called Stanky and Maxvill was on a plane for Indianapolis within 48 hours.

Maxvill wasn't your typical minor-league baseball player. He had a degree in electrical engineering from Washington University in St. Louis. He was serious about baseball, too, which was obvious as soon as he showed up in my office to sign his contract. That formality complete, he said matter-of-factly, "How do you get to the clubhouse from here?" He was anxious to put on the Indians uniform and get to work.

He played in 45 games, hit .285, was outstanding defensively, and helped spark the team to a winning record. But the Cardinals recalled him on July 31, the day of the deadline for recalling an optioned player. Maxvill would have had to stay with us the rest of the season if he hadn't been recalled.

Maxvill helped spark the Cardinals, too, all the way from sixth place in the National League to the pennant and the World Series championship. He was a utility infielder as well as an outfielder for them, then played all seven games at second base against the Yankees in the Series. He replaced Julian Javier, who had to sit out the series (except for a pinch-running appearance) because of a bruised hip.

Just think, Maxvill went from languishing on the bench as a shortstop on a minor-league team in Jacksonville to starring in the World Series for the Cardinals. He only batted .200 in the Series, but he played great defense.

The Indians, ironically, replaced Maxvill with Cooter Veal, and he performed capably. We didn't win a championship, but I was happy for Maxvill because he was an overachiever who got the most out of his ability. He played in the Majors until 1975, when he was 36 years old, and later became the Cardinals' general manager.

We helped him advance his career, and that's one of the pleasures of being a minor-league general manager. ⬤

Dave DeBusschere's last professional baseball game was with the Indianapolis Indians before he focused on a Hall of Fame basketball career.

DAVE DEBUSSCHERE

D ave DeBusschere was a rare athlete, one of 13 men who have played professional basketball and Major League Baseball. At 6-foot-6, he had starred in both sports at the University of Detroit and, upon graduation in 1962, was drafted by both the Chicago White Sox of MLB and Detroit Pistons of the NBA.

The general consensus among baseball people was that he preferred basketball, but the White Sox gave him a $60,000 signing bonus in hopes of convincing him to concentrate on baseball. He played the 1962 – 63 season for the Pistons, averaging 12.7 points and 8.7 rebounds and earning all-rookie honors, and pitched for the White Sox the rest of that year. He threw a complete-game shutout for them in August against the Cleveland Indians, but came to Indianapolis in 1964 after an injury shortened his basketball season to 15 games.

He went 15 – 8, with a 3.93 ERA, and was a good hitter for a pitcher with a .222 batting average. The Pistons made him their player-coach the following season at age 24, when he averaged 16.7 points and 11.1 rebounds. He returned to Indianapolis in '65, going 15 – 12 with a 3.65 ERA. Frustrated by the White Sox' refusal to call him up, he retired from baseball as soon as the Indians' season ended to focus on basketball.

He later became a member of the New York Knicks' championship teams of 1970 and '73, was selected to play in eight All-Star games, became commissioner of the American Basketball Association in its last season (1975 – 76), and was voted into the Naismith Basketball Hall of Fame in 1983.

His final appearance in a baseball uniform came in our 5 – 4 win over Arkansas on September 6. He allowed four hits and three runs in eight innings, but didn't get a victory in the 10-inning game. Only 662 fans watched the afternoon game at Victory Field. It was a humble exit from baseball for him, but he still had a notable career in his "second sport."

I have no doubt he could have made it as a major-league pitcher, but ultimately he did what nearly everyone expected he would do: play basketball. The White Sox—and Indians—were lucky to have him, and as his NBA career blossomed, it became a point of pride among our fans that he had worn the Indians uniform.

He didn't forget about us, either. One day in 1975 when he was in Indianapolis while serving as commissioner of the American Basketball Association, he walked into my office at Bush Stadium unannounced. He didn't stay long, but apparently wanted to rekindle some memories. ●

UNHAPPY ENDING TO A HAPPY ERA

The Indianapolis Indians' six-year affiliation with the Chicago White Sox ended in 1967, after a frustrating season for both sides. They were trying to win the American League pennant, and we were trying to win the Eastern Division of the Pacific Coast League that season. As it turned out, we both fell short. The White Sox finished three games behind Boston and we finished 8 1/2 games behind San Diego.

We were within striking distance most of the season, but the White Sox kept recalling players from our team—64 times in all. We routinely have twice that many today, but it was excessive compared to other teams at the time. The local media reacted negatively to the constant call-ups, and the fans followed their lead.

Our frustration boiled over on July 31. San Diego, the team we were battling for the Eastern Division lead in the PCL, came to Bush Stadium for a crucial four-game series. The Indians won the first game, 6 – 2, but afterward the White Sox instructed us to send second baseman Lorenzo "Chico" Fernandez to Evansville, their Double-A affiliate. Evansville was 1 1/2 games back of the lead in its league and owned his contract, but he had been promised he would not be blocked from advancing to a higher classification as long as he was playing regularly. He had played in every game for us and was hitting .251 while playing great defense, with just four errors all season, so he was vital to our title hopes.

After the game, manager Don Gutteridge and all the players gathered in my office to put their name to a protest to be wired to Glenn Miller, Chicago's farm director. The petition stated their belief that they could win the division if Fernandez was kept on the roster.

"What are they trying to do to us?" one anonymous player told *The Indianapolis News*. "First they take away our guys to help the White Sox win a pennant, and now they're taking 'em to help Evansville win. What about us? We've got a chance to win, too."

Our fans were so angry some of them later made a dummy of White Sox manager Eddie Stanky and hung him in effigy from the stadium girders.

Fernandez was angry, too.

"I play and work hard here," he said. "I think I helped the club. Now I have to go. I'm very depressed. I don't want to leave this fine bunch of players. But I guess that's the way it has to be. I don't think I'll play baseball next year."

The Indians won again the next night without Fernandez, but lost their next two games to San Diego in extra innings to split the series. We dropped quickly from pennant contention after that and finished second, 8 1/2 games back in the East.

Fernandez was replaced by Joe Faraci, who had been playing for Syracuse in the International League. Faraci hit just .118 in 22 games for the Indians the remainder of that season and then left baseball.

Fernandez, however, didn't follow up on his threat to retire. Baltimore acquired him the following season and he made their roster out of spring training, but he appeared in only 24 games and managed just two singles in 18 at-bats. He finished his baseball career by playing in four games for Rochester in the International League in 1969.

We'll never know what would have happened if Fernandez had

The decision to demote Chico Fernandez to Double-A might have cost Indianapolis a pennant in 1967.

been allowed to finish the season with us. But in the bigger picture, the White Sox might have done us a favor.

We announced the termination of our working agreement with them on the last day of the season, a decision reached by mutual agreement. We had enjoyed a successful run with them by winning pennants in 1962 and '63, finishing second in '64, third in '65 and '66, and second in '67. But it was time to move on. And that turned out to be a good thing.

DON ZIMMER

Don Zimmer was employed in professional baseball as a player, coach, manager, or other position for 65 years, from 1949 until he died in 2014. So, it seems inevitable he passed through Indianapolis at some point. He managed the Indians in 1968, the season in which we began a renewed affiliation with the Cincinnati Reds. He was a native of Cincinnati and had been a player-manager the previous season at the age of 36 for the Reds' Triple-A and Double-A affiliates in Knoxville and Buffalo.

It didn't go well. We finished 66 – 78 in our last season in the Pacific Coast League, 27 games out of first in the Eastern Division. I don't think anyone could have made that team a championship contender, but Zimmer failed to impress. He was a raw, hard-nosed young man trying to figure out how to go about the job.

Ownie Bush was ready to fire him in August, when the season had become a lost cause. He and I had a meeting with the Reds' farm director, Chief Bender, between games of a doubleheader in August to discuss Zimmer's fate. Bender was willing to make a change but not really wanting to, and I was able to steer Ownie away from the idea. I told him before the meeting that whoever the Reds sent to replace Zimmer wasn't likely to be any better, and I reminded him that he had always said teams rarely benefited from changing managers during the season.

Zimmer was released upon the conclusion of the Indians' final game of the season in September. It came as no surprise to him, because he had asked me whether we planned to bring him back before the team's final West Coast road trip. I told him no, and he had a job lined up with San Diego's expansion franchise before the season ended, courtesy of his longtime friend Buzzie Bavasi.

To his credit, he continued to manage our team as seriously as he had all season after learning of his fate. But our attendance in the season's final game, 772, reflected the depths to which we had fallen.

Zimmer suffered two major concussions during his playing career as the result of beanings. The first one occurred in 1953 when he was 22 years old and playing for the Triple-A American Association team in St. Paul, Minnesota. That life-threatening incident left him in a coma for 13 days and led to the introduction of batting helmets to the game. He suffered another concussion while playing for the Brooklyn Dodgers in 1956 when a fastball hit him in the cheekbone.

He got a lot of comedic material out of telling people he had a plate in his head as a result of his injuries, but it wasn't true. He told me as much. But he did have four holes drilled in his skull during his first surgery, and he did suffer from severe headaches periodically while with the Indians. At times while I was talking with him, he would drop his head into his hands because of the pain.

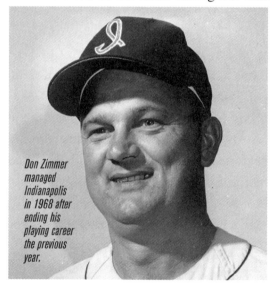

Don Zimmer managed Indianapolis in 1968 after ending his playing career the previous year.

He wound up managing San Diego's Single-A affiliate in Key West, Florida in 1969, then moved up to their Triple-A team in Salt Lake City in 1970. He joined Montreal as a third-base coach in 1971 and worked in the major-leagues for the rest of his life. He managed four teams and coached for seven others.

Although he became a beloved figure in the game because of his humble nature, sense of humor, and roly-poly appearance, nobody who knew him during his time as the Indianapolis manager would have predicted that kind of career for him.

Temperamental Vern Rapp managed the Indianapolis Indians from 1969-75, an eternity in minor league baseball.

VERN RAPP

Vern Rapp's seven-season run as the Indianapolis Indians' manager is the longest in franchise history, and an eternity in the world of minor league baseball. Hired in 1969, he became the first of our managers since 1959 to survive more than one season. He'll go down as one of the most talented and memorable managers in minor league baseball as well. ● Vern was hired after Don Zimmer's Indians team finished 66 – 78 in 1968. The natural hire would have been Sparky Anderson, who had managed minor-league teams to championships the previous four years, including the Reds' Double-A affiliate in Ashville, North Carolina in 1968. Vern, however, was hired out of the St. Louis farm system.

Vern and Sparky had been good friends and had a lot in common. Both had lengthy minor-league playing careers but failed to reach the Majors. Both became managers at a young age and worked their way up through the minors. They had an agreement that whichever one of them became a major-league manager first would hire the other as a coach. That turned out to be Sparky, who took over the Reds in 1970, but he didn't hire Vern for his staff.

That angered Vern, but it turned out to be a great thing for the Indians. We won two division championships and had two second-place finishes during his run from 1969 – 75, during which he was voted Manager of the Year twice.

I discovered quickly that Vern had a Jekyll and Hyde element to his personality. In uniform, he was tough and temperamental. Out of uniform, he was calm and considerate. A sportswriter who covered his managing career in the Texas League prior to coming to the Indians once wrote, "Before a ballgame, he is as friendly as a collie dog. Once in a game, he'll use anything up to poison gas to try to beat you. He is a tough loser, and in the heat of battle, he can erupt like a volcano."

Needless to say, whenever I needed to talk business with him, I tried to wait until he was out of uniform. I loved working with him, though, and will always be sorry we couldn't win a league championship for him. But we came close, and I enjoyed a lot of exciting moments with him—some of which the fans never witnessed.

There was the time, for example, we had a sponsored doubleheader, one of the nights we depended on financially because of the guaranteed revenue. The chairman of the sponsoring company asked for an extra five minutes between games so he could introduce a few people during the on-field ceremony. I wasn't about to say no.

When the first game ended, I immediately called Vern down in the dugout and told him we needed 20 minutes instead of 15 before starting the second game.

"That's too goddamn long!" he shouted, and slammed the phone down. We took an extra five, anyway.

Another evening, we were playing our annual exhibition against the Reds, with 14,000 fans in the stands. This obviously was a crucial night for us, sometimes determining whether our bottom line was red or black at the end of the season.

Several of the Reds had showered and were in street clothes in the later innings, and Sparky wound up short of players. He had taken pitcher Jack Billingham out of the game, but wanted to put him back in, in left field, to finish the game.

When the umpire took the request to Vern he said no, rules were rules. It wasn't long before Sparky and Vern, the former friends, were arguing back and forth through the umpire. I don't recall if Billingham was allowed back into the game, but afterward the Reds' farm director, Sheldon "Chief" Bender was fuming.

"We're over here to help the Indians, what the hell difference does it make if we put a player back in the game?!" he shouted.

Vern's response was brief and blunt: "Tough shitskie!"

Vern never was opposed to an argument. One day I received a bulletin that the scheduled umpire was unavailable for a game. The replacement was to be Frannie Walsh, a longtime umpire who had worked mostly in the minor leagues. Vern knew him from their time together in the Texas League, where Vern had managed for four seasons before coming to the Indians.

Vern was excited when I told him Walsh would be working the game.

"Frannie Walsh! He's a great guy! I love Frannie Walsh!"

During the game that night, Vern was itching for a way to show his love for Frannie. When he finally found a call he could argue, he came charging out of the dugout. The two stood nose to nose screaming at one another, their heads bobbing up and down, as if they wanted to kill one another. Frannie never did kick him out, though. He knew Vern was just having fun with him. They were like professional wrestlers, putting on a show for the fans.

Vern was like that. He was friends with a lot of the umpires, but would have long and dramatic arguments with them during games. He pressed the envelope in the language he used, though, and I often warned him against that. He didn't do us much good if he was out of the game, so I wanted him to be more careful with his choice of words.

One year in our league meeting, though, the topic of manager-umpire disputes came up and the league's supervisor of umpires shrugged it off, saying, "It's just baseball talk." Vern looked over his shoulder at me and said, "See, I told you so."

Vern's anger wasn't always a put-on, though. He was a Korean War

veteran and never backed down from a fight. Even a fistfight. He was a "player's manager" in my opinion, one who usually took the side of the player in disputes with management, but he wasn't afraid to confront a player when he felt it necessary.

Pedro Borbón, who would go on to a 12-year major-league career in which he won 64 percent of his games as a relief pitcher, played for the Indians in 1970 and '71. He and Vern were both hard-nosed, emotional men who clashed frequently, so one night in 1971, they decided to settle their differences man-to-man.

According to a story relayed to me many years later by our third baseman at the time, Dick Kenworthy, Borbón met Vern in his office, a small room barely big enough to contain a desk. They went at it, bouncing off the walls and making all kinds of racket while the players stood in the locker room and listened, silent and wide-eyed.

Who won the fight?

Vern did, according to Kenworthy.

Remember, though, Vern was a different man in street clothes. We had another temperamental pitcher in the 1973 and '74 seasons in Joaquín Andujar, who would have a 13-year major-league career and play in four All-Star games. Joaquin had taken a leave because of a death in his family and returned a day late, but we had let it go.

One night after a game, Vern brought him up to my office, which was unusual because he usually settled all disputes with players himself. I don't recall the exact nature of their argument, but at one point Joaquin said, "You guys don't like me!"

That's when I became angry.

"What are you talking about, Joaquín?" I said. "You just had a death in your family and we let you go home and you took an extra day and I never said a word about it. We didn't fine you and I didn't tell the Reds you were late, so don't say 'You guys don't like me.'"

Joaquin looked at me and said, "Well, you're OK, but he doesn't like me, and never has."

Vern just sat there, completely docile. That surprised me. But then again, he was out of uniform.

Vern left the Indians after the 1975 season to take over Denver's Triple-A team. I couldn't blame him. He was angry that he hadn't been hired to fill an open position on Sparky Anderson's coaching staff. Anderson was entrenched as Cincinnati's manager at the time, so that avenue to the Majors was blocked. Vern had played for Denver from 1958 – 60 and kept a home in the area since then. It provided him a chance to go "home" and perhaps improve his odds of reaching the Majors.

He made a wise choice. Denver went 86 – 50 the following season and won the league championship. Vern even inserted himself as a pinch-hitter in one regular-season game. He was 48 years old, but got a base hit and drove in a run.

That season led to his big break, becoming manager of the St. Louis Cardinals. His timing wasn't great, though, taking over after Red Schoendienst's 12-year run. Schoendienst, who led the Cardinals to a World Series championship in 1967, had taken a relaxed approach with his players. Transitioning to a disciplinarian and war veteran like Vern was bound to cause conflicts with some of the players about issues such as facial hair and how a uniform should be worn.

The Cardinals improved by 11 games from the previous season and finished third in their division in 1977, but Vern was fired after 16 games in the 1978 season. He then coached with Montreal from 1979 – 83. He planned to retire after the '83 season, but unexpectedly got another chance when the Reds hired him to manage in 1984. He was fired in August of that season, however, in favor of Pete Rose, who took over as player-manager.

Vern was 56 years old by then, so he retired from baseball. He didn't go quite as far as he wanted as the Indianapolis Indians' manager, but he'll always go down as one of the best in our franchise's history. ◉

PARTY ANIMALS

T he Indianapolis Indians held a team party for several years in August, usually after a Sunday afternoon game. It was a tradition that predated my time as general manager, because I recall that at my first spring training in 1961, one of the players asked me when it would be held that year. It was a simple and casual gathering, basically an opportunity for the players to relax and get to know some of the important people outside their clubhouse a little better, such as front office employees, members of our board of directors and sponsors. Someone such as our groundskeeper Ike Ives would help me ice down beer and soft drinks, and we'd have a catered fried chicken dinner from Jug Eckert.

It usually came off without a problem, but you never know what might happen when you bring professional athletes together.

There was the time in 1969, for example, when outfielder Mike de la Hoz decided to dive into the swimming pool at the home of Edwin T. French, a member of our board. He was being egged on by teammates to get into the pool, so finally gave in. Only problem was, he dove into the shallow end, cracked his head on the concrete bottom and suffered a serious head injury.

Mike was a 30-year-old veteran of 493 major-league games at that time. He had peaked when he hit .294 for the Milwaukee Braves in 1964 and was trying to work his way back to the Majors. He hit .355 for us that season, but only played in 95 of our 140 games.

Mike did make one plate appearance for the Reds in September, and struck out. That was his last appearance in a major-league game.

We also lost two other valuable outfielders that season, Clyde Mashore and Stan Swanson, to National Guard duty. This was during the peak of the Vietnam War, and many athletes had to serve in the Guard for stretches of time. Mashore hit .285 in 116 games, and Swanson hit .291 in 103 games.

We also lost a promising shortstop, Frank Duffy, for two weeks to attend a two-week Marine summer camp. He would go on to play 10 major-league seasons.

Worst of all, we only had Hal McRae—who had hit .295 and played in the All-Star game the previous season—for 17 games in the '69 season as he recovered from a broken leg suffered in winter ball.

Needless to say our record suffered from the absence of all those players. We finished 74 – 66, third in the American Association.

In minor league baseball, however, losing a player creates an opportunity for another player, and often creates intriguing possibilities.

From the ruins of our losses in 1969, a future star emerged. Dave Concepción was called up from the Reds' Double-A affiliate in Ashville, North Carolina to replace Duffy and hit .341 for us in 42 games. He made his debut on July 26 and contributed two singles and a stolen base. He was moved to second base, third base, and the outfield after Duffy returned because he was too good to keep out of the lineup.

He was too good to keep in the minors, too. He spent the following 19 seasons playing for the Reds, earning nine All-Star selections and five Gold Gloves.

Another team party in 1974 *nearly* got someone hurt. We had been no-hit on that Sunday afternoon by Iowa's Butch Stinson, a 22-year-old unknown to us before the game, who never did make it to the Majors. It was a crucial game for us, so Vern Rapp wasn't feeling like going to a party afterward.

He did, though, and was challenged to a one-on-one basketball game by Pat Zachry, one of our promising pitchers. Vern was 46 years old at the time, but he was a tough guy and, that day, in a foul mood. He and Zachry both were extremely competitive and the game became so physical they nearly came to blows.

The hoop remained in the driveway at our future parties, but we conveniently "lost" the basketball. And after a while, we stopped having the parties altogether.

The players loved them in the 1960s and 1970s, but as the years went by, they gradually lost interest. ●

By 1971 Max had been on the job as general manager for a decade.

1971

The 1971 season was one of the most memorable for me, thanks mostly to Vern Rapp. But also to Jim McIntyre. Rapp's third team in Indianapolis was the best of the seven he managed for us, well-stocked with promising players in a Cincinnati Reds organization that was gathering the talent that would win World Series titles in 1975 and '76. Pedro Borbón (12 – 6), Ross Grimsley (6 – 0), Dick Baney (9 – 4), Ed Sprague (9 – 6), Dave Tomlin (7 – 4), and Milt Wilcox (8 – 5) led an outstanding pitching staff, and Kurt Bevacqua (.302), Bill Plummer (17 home runs), and Willie Smith (.351) were major contributors to the offense

The Indians finished 84 – 55 that season, easily the best record in the American Association and 13 1/2 games ahead of second-place Iowa in the Eastern Division. We faced Western Division champion Denver, which won 73 games, for the league championship.

The first three games of the best-of-seven series were played at Bush Stadium. The Indians won each of the first two, 3 – 2, but dropped Game Three in 10 innings, 6 – 3. Denver outfielder Richie Scheinblum threw out two of our runners at home plate in that game, including Dick Kenworthy in the ninth inning.

That play represented a rare managerial mistake on Vern's part. Kenworthy was a 30-year-old third baseman who had played 125 games for the White Sox between 1962 and '68. He was hardly fleet of foot, and was gunned down by Scheinblum trying to score from second base on Jim Qualls' single to right.

More than 25 years later, Kenworthy worked as a host in the "Indians Suite" at our new downtown ballpark. One night he admitted, "Vern should have run for me."

Denver won Game Four back in Denver, 6 – 5, to tie the series at two games apiece. Indianapolis scored five runs in the ninth inning, three of them on a triple by Willie Smith, but failed to get the sixth run home when Plummer struck out to end the game.

Game Five was postponed a day to September 8 by rain, which turned out to be fateful. The Indians won, 10 – 2, to take a 3 – 2 series lead, but that set up a most unusual finish to the series. The NFL's Denver Broncos were to begin their season on September 19th and needed 10 days to sod the field and add bleachers to the stadium. That meant our series with Denver would have to end on September 9, with a split doubleheader if necessary.

If the Indians won the first game of the day, we would be champions. If we lost, Game Seven would be played that evening after a break of a few hours.

Denver came back from a 2– 0 deficit to win Game Six, 4 – 2, and then won Game Seven, 5 – 2. It was a tough way to finish after so obviously being the best team during the regular season.

Vern didn't go down quietly, though. He was ejected by umpire Fred Blandford in the eighth inning of the afternoon game and by Dick Sievers in the fifth inning of the night game. I asked him afterward what he had done to be kicked out and he said, "I don't know why he would do that, all I did was call him a bastard."

Vern provided some humor for the Denver fans in one of the games by walking as slowly as possible to the clubhouse in right-center field after his ejection. Once there, he opened the door and began watching the game from inside the room. Fans began shouting, and the umpire told him to close the door. Vern might have closed it once or twice, but quickly reopened it. The umpire finally walked all the way out to confront him, but as soon as he reached the clubhouse door Vern slammed it in his face.

Vern took the losses hard, though. When Reds general manager Bob Howsam told him afterward that he had done a great job and began talking about the following season, Vern broke down crying.

"Go ahead, don't hold back," Howsam said. "You have nothing to be ashamed of."

Everyone felt crushed by the way the season ended. It had been a magical ride until the very end. Willie Smith personified our season. A converted pitcher, his batting average had exceeded .400 much of the season until falling to .351 at the end. He batted .296 in the playoffs but left 15 baserunners stranded in the four games in Denver. He approached me in the clubhouse to tell me he had never enjoyed a season as much as that one, and he told my wife Judy later that evening he had never been as emotionally involved in games before that season. He was 32 at the time and had been playing professionally since 1960. He finished that season with Cincinnati, then played two more seasons in Japan before retiring.

Along with the emotional agony of falling short in those final two games in Denver, I suffered some physical pain as well.

During Game Three in Indianapolis, I went to the Perry Room at Bush Stadium to make a cold meat sandwich. I don't know what I bit into, but I broke off a tooth on the side of my mouth. The jagged edge of the damaged tooth rubbed against my cheek when I talked, and it hurt terribly.

When I arrived home that night I received a call from Katie McIntyre, wife of our radio broadcaster, Jim. She told me Jim had been hospitalized and wouldn't be able to make the trip to Denver the following day. Suddenly, I needed a broadcaster. I made a call to Tom Hession, a teacher and football/baseball coach at Shelbyville High School as well as a state senator. He had broadcast Indianapolis Indians games from 1966 to '69, but he wasn't able to go.

I made calls to other people, too. I wasn't trying to find another Vin Scully, just someone better than Max Schumacher. It was impossible to find anyone able to stop whatever they were doing and fly to Denver the next day, so I had to take the job myself, bad tooth and all.

I found an engineer in Denver who got me on the air and in and out of station breaks. He tapped me on the shoulder every time we needed to break. I don't know how I got through Game Four with so much pain in my mouth, and I can only imagine what that broadcast sounded like back in Indianapolis.

Someone made an appointment for me with a dentist in Denver the following day and the problem was corrected, but it still wasn't easy broadcasting the remaining games. For some reason, some Denver fans were sitting in the booth where I was calling the game and making all kinds of racket. I politely told them, "I'm sorry, but I'm a rookie broadcaster and need all the help I can get. Could you please cheer a little more quietly?" They were nice about it and quieted down.

The only good thing to come out of that experience for me is that no tapes of my performance exist. 🔘

GENE LOCKLEAR

Some losing seasons bring great performances, and unexpected accomplishments. ● Gene Locklear played just one season in Indianapolis, in 1972, when we finished 22 games out of first place, but the 22-year-old outfielder led the American Association with a .325 batting average and was named to the All-Star team. ● He made an impression another way as well.

Locklear, a full-blooded Lumbee Indian, showed up in my office one day early in the season with a business proposal. He had been fined $50 by the league office for an infraction neither he nor I remember. He offered to paint our weather-beaten centerfield teepee, which looked, as he put it, "a bit shabby," asking only that I buy the paint and pay him $50 to cover the fine.

I immediately agreed, and he took care of the task on the afternoon of June 6. He did a great job, turning the teepee into a work of art. Then he went out that night and collected three hits and scored two runs in a 9 – 5 victory over Oklahoma City.

Locklear went on to play in five major-league seasons for the Reds, Padres, and Yankees. His best season was 1975 when he played in 100 games for the Padres and batted .321. His last appearance in the Majors came in 1977 when he played in one game for the Yankees—and had three singles in five at-bats. He completed his playing career the following year in Japan.

He went on to become an accomplished artist, with works encompassing sports and Indian heritage. He has a doctorate in Fine Arts from the University of North Carolina and has been commissioned to paint portraits of several baseball players as well as golfers Tiger Woods and Phil Mickelson, NASCAR driver Rusty Wallace, and basketball center Bill Walton.

The teepee that Gene painted in 1972 eventually had to be replaced. We later tried to move the replacement to our new downtown ballpark when we left Bush Stadium, but it came apart and was unusable.

We bought a new one and placed it in left-centerfield beyond the outfield, in the lawn area, but eventually it became weather-beaten as well. It was decided not to replace that one because it was becoming too much to fuss with.

Indian references have been controversial in sports. Some colleges, such as St. John's and Stanford, have changed their nicknames from "Redmen" and "Indians." In major-league baseball, the Cleveland Indians' logo is of Chief Wahoo, a smiling caricature of an Indian face, while the Atlanta Braves have the "chop" cheer, which imitates a tomahawk dropping. Some people interpret them to be disrespectful to the Native American culture, and when controversies flared, I often received a call from a media outlet wondering if we were considering changing our nickname.

I always replied that we would consider doing so only if the name of the city and state in which we play changed. Indians is certainly an appropriate nickname for a team in Indianapolis, Indiana.

I don't believe we've ever exploited the nickname or done anything that reflects poorly on the Native American culture. Our mascot, Rowdie, is a bear. We did once have a fan, Pearce Relander, a Caucasian man, who was a great admirer of Indian culture and came to games dressed as a Native American. He carried a pocketful of Buffalo nickels to hand out to kids, but he wasn't paid and he didn't perform in any way. He just settled into a seat and watched the game.

If Gene Locklear wasn't offended by our use of a teepee to add some flavor to our ballpark, that's good enough for me. ●

Resuming an affiliation with Cincinnati brought many great players to the Indianapolis Indians, including George Foster.

GEORGE FOSTER

R eturning to the Cincinnati Reds as their Triple-A affiliate in 1968 was fortunate, as it enabled us to help develop some of the stars of their Big Red Machine teams of the 1970s. ● The Reds were unhappy with the relationship with their Triple-A affiliate in Buffalo, which had finished one-half game out of last place in the International League in 1967, so we were able to sign a two-year contract with them.

Our unhappy parting in 1961 seemed like ancient history by that time. The issue of how much we should pay in salaries was no longer a concern, as salary obligations for minor-league affiliates had been standardized. Our timing was good, too. The Reds had a new, aggressive management team and were headed toward the greatest run of success in their history. We were happy to be along for the ride.

Neither Pete Rose, Johnny Bench, Tony Perez, nor Joe Morgan played for us on their way up to Cincinnati. We missed Bench by just one year, as he played 98 games for Buffalo in 1967. Some of the Reds' other stars first wore an Indianapolis Indians uniform, though, including Dave Concepción, Bernie Carbo, Pedro Borbón, Dan Driessen, Ross Grimsley, Ken Griffey Sr., Ray Knight, and Rawly Eastwick.

George Foster was perhaps the most memorable of all.

Foster played for the Indians in 1973 after the Reds acquired him in a trade with San Francisco for Frank Duffy, but to that point he had not showed the kind of power that would become the foundation of his major-league career.

I went with our manager, Vern Rapp, to the Reds' spring-training site at the University of South Florida in Tampa before the 1973 season. We wanted to meet Foster, and found him in his hotel room. He was so bashful he peeked at us through a small crack in the door and was so soft-spoken that it was difficult to hear him.

Foster hit some home runs in spring training but was the last player cut by the Reds. He had played in parts of five major-league seasons by the time he got to us, but still wasn't quite ready. He blasted long balls in batting practice after the season began, but he wasn't showing much power in games because he was pressing.

Around mid-May, Vern moved Foster from fifth in the batting order to the leadoff position and told him to just play pepper—stick out his bat and try to hit the ball past the pitcher without worrying about home runs. Just focus on making contact. Foster soon began hitting again, and eventually showed some power.

He hit 15 homers that season while batting .262, and hit .311 over his last five weeks with us before the Reds called him up in September. He never saw the minors again. He played for Cincinnati through the 1981 season, was traded to the New York Mets before the '82 season, and played the final 15 games of his career with the White Sox in 1986 at age 37.

He was voted the National League's Most Valuable Player in 1977 when he hit 52 home runs and played in five All-Star games, earning MVP honors in one of them. Best of all, he played on two championship teams with the Reds.

I'd like to think Vern Rapp deserves at least some credit for all that success. ●

BATBOYS

aseball batboys go back to the nineteenth century, and the Indianapolis Indians are no different than any other professional team. We've had them for as long as anyone can remember. ● The method of selecting our batboys changed when the Cleveland Indians took over ownership of the Indians' minor-league franchise in 1952. In an effort to publicize the team, they enlisted the local newspapers to participate in projects related to the team. *The Indianapolis Star* began sponsoring a batboy contest that year, while the News sponsored an annual clinic for kids. Those programs continued for a few decades, but were eventually discontinued.

The *Star* published an entry form early in March and invited boys to apply by writing an essay of 150 words or less explaining why they wanted the job. Ten finalists were selected and brought in for interviews at the ballpark. I would be joined by the field manager and a representative from the Star and together we would select a winner.

It was a two-year obligation, with the winner working for the visiting team the first year and for the Indians the second year. The winner received a wrist watch from the *Star* and every student at his school

A batboy's varied duties included helping remove the tarp when necessary, as seen in this shot from the mid-1960s.

was offered a free ticket to a game. He was allowed to go on a road trip with the team during his second season, and room with one of the (more responsible) players, and then when his term concluded, was awarded a $400 check to be applied toward college expenses. I'm not sure about the early years, but later the batboy received $2 per game, and more if he helped roll out the tarp when there was a rain delay.

The first *Star* contest in 1952 drew 350 entries. The winner, Ray Oyler, was a student at Cathedral High School who went on to play in the major leagues. He joined the Detroit Tigers as a good-field, no-hit shortstop in 1965 and was a member of their 1968 World Series championship team. He only appeared in the Series as a late-inning defensive replacement, however, because of his anemic bat. He hit .135 that season, thought to be the worst average in major-league history for players appearing in more than 100 games.

He also played for the Seattle Pilots expansion team and the California Angels before retiring in 1970 with a career batting average of .175.

Oyler, who was 15 years old and stood 5-foot-1 during his seasons as a batboy, worked out regularly with the Indians. He made a 15-day road trip with the team in July that included stops in four cities, and the *Star* published his written account of that trip. He even played second base in the ninth inning of an exhibition game in Green Bay, but didn't have a fielding chance.

The players took up a collection so he would have spending money after Coach Johnny Hutchings addressed the team on the train and declared him to be the best batboy in the league.

Despite his poor batting average in the Majors, Oyler was a standout all-around prep athlete. He was an excellent baseball player, of course, but also quarterbacked the school's city championship football team, and was a star basketball player. Hopefully his season with the Indians contributed to his baseball career, although perhaps he should have taken part in pregame batting practice more often.

While none of the other Indians batboys have gone on to major-league careers, many have done well professionally and benefited from the experience. It's a great opportunity for a young kid to see how hard professional athletes work and how they interact with one another. Working as a batboy is humbling and requires a lot of effort. But the kids are always treated well by the players and other adults if they have a good attitude, so it's a great education.

Mark Storen, a batboy in the 1973 and '74 seasons, became a popular media figure in Indianapolis in later years, under the name Mark Patrick. He first applied for the job as a 12-year-old in 1971 and was accepted as one of the ten finalists. But when he was asked in the interview if his parents would be able to provide transportation to and from games, he answered honestly and said no, his dad worked a lot of hours and his mother didn't have a car.

Two years later he once again became a finalist and this time knew to commit his parents to the task and work out the details later. "They would love to bring me to the games," he recalls saying. "No problem at all. My mom has a car now, too."

Storen describes his years as a batboy as providing an "amazing education" about baseball. One of his favorite memories involves the game Denny McLain pitched for Iowa during McLain's comeback attempt in '73. McLain had nothing left on his fastball by then, and was practically lobbing pitches to the plate.

Finally, as McLain was catching the toss back from the catcher, a fan shouted, "C'mon McLain, you can throw harder than that! Put some heat on it!"

McLain dropped the ball and his glove on the ground as soon as he heard the plea, then stepped off the mound and shouted, "If I could throw the ball harder than that, don't you think I'd be doing it?!"

One of the other Iowa players Storen met that season was Mark Marquess, who doubled as a coach for the Oaks in 1973. Marquess went on to become the head baseball coach at Stanford from 1977 to 2017 and coached Storen's son, Drew, who has gone on to a major-league pitching career with Washington, Toronto, Seattle, and Cincinnati.

Drew has worked some games as a batboy, too. The trainer while Mark was a batboy for the Indians, Ron McClain, later became the

Montreal Expos' trainer. Years later, he arranged for Drew to work as a batboy for some of the Expos games in Cincinnati and St. Louis.

Mark's successor was Ken Loudenback, a batboy in the 1974 and '75 seasons. He impressed us in his interview when our manager, Vern Rapp, asked him if he would be willing to cut his hair if selected.

"If you let me be a batboy for the Indianapolis Indians, I'll get a Mohawk," he said.

Ken's mother was a single parent raising four children, so Ken said he would take a bus to the games from his home in Eagledale about five miles away and find a ride home afterward. He wound up getting rides to the games from neighbors most of the time, but we were impressed with his initiative and fortitude.

He also benefited from the relationships he formed as a batboy. He was a "latchkey" kid because his mother had to work to support the family, but the players, front office personnel and even fans became a second family to him. Dave Revering attended his eighth grade graduation ceremony and he was particularly close to Ed Armbrister and Ken Griffey as well.

Ken made a 15-day road trip through Tulsa, Oklahoma City, and Omaha with the team, where he saw firsthand all that goes into playing the game. The Indians won a championship in1974 and were a winning team again in '75, so he got to see all the factors that go into being successful. He later graduated with honors with a business degree from Indiana University, and, after a successful career in business, became a pastor.

"I don't know if any of that would have happened if not for my experience as a batboy," he says. "I got a lot of good examples. It set me up for the rest of my life."

We've had few problems with batboys over the years. Any kid who has the initiative to enter the contest and go through the selection process is likely to be a cut above average. I do recall one instance, though, when a batboy quit his position in August because he could earn more money de-tasseling corn. I called his father, who was an executive for Coca Cola, but Dad let the boy have his way. I thought that would have been a great opportunity to enforce the point that you should stick with your commitments and not leave an employer or friends before the job is complete.

In later years, we included girls as candidates for the batboy position. *The Star* changed the terminology from batboy to "bat handler," but it didn't work out. We didn't attract entries from many girls, if any, and boys were turned off. We barely received enough entries to have 10 finalists that year. I think every kid who entered that year got an interview. The Star cancelled the promotion the following year for "lack of interest."

We ran into a problem in later years with the federal government.

A woman who came in sporadically to clean up our offices had a fallout with a man who was, or had been, her husband. To get back at her, he reported her for using their children to help her clean. She brought them with her to work sometimes and might occasionally ask one of them to bring a bucket over to her or some simple task as that, but they weren't working for her.

I received a visit from a woman named Mary Ellen from the local division of the U.S. Department of Labor. Her investigation led to a conversation about how late our batboys worked at night.

I told her that for a young teenager who didn't have transportation and hadn't discovered girls, being a batboy was a great opportunity. I even offered to let her talk to some former batboys for their feedback.

Her response: "I'm not interested in anything like that. I'm only interested in their age and how late they work at night."

From that point on, we began to hire older kids, age 16 – 18, who could drive themselves to work, and pay them an hourly wage. The job isn't as romantic as it once was for a young boy, but the kids still benefit from doing it, I think. Even if they don't become major-league players. ◉

MARK FIDRYCH

One of the best things about Triple-A baseball is that fans get to see rising stars on their way to the major leagues. Sometimes they also get to see players at the other end of their career, as former major leaguers trying to recover their skills. ● That had been the case when Denny McLain pitched against the Indians in 1973, and it was true for Mark Fidrych as well.

Fidrych pitched once against the Indians on his way up to Detroit while playing for Evansville. Having just been called up from Detroit's Double-A team in Montgomery, Alabama, he started the first game of a doubleheader on August 22, 1975. He pitched 4 1/3 innings and allowed two runs, both earned, but did not get the decision in Evansville's 6 – 2 victory.

He became Major League Baseball's biggest star the following season.

After earning a spot on Detroit's roster in spring training with a contract for the minimum salary, he went 19 – 9, led the American League in ERA (2.34), and was voted Rookie of the Year. He won people over with more than his performance, though. He stood 6-foot-3 and was nicknamed "The Bird" because of his resemblance to the Big Bird character on the Sesame Street children's television show. He had long, curly hair that stuck out from under his cap and an eccentric nature that captivated fans. He often talked to the ball between pitches, strutted around the mound after outs, and sometimes got on his hands and knees to groom the mound to his liking. He also had a humble, innocent personality that made him popular with everyone.

Fidrych suffered a torn rotator cuff in a game with the Tigers on July 4, 1977, and was never the same. He last pitched in the Majors for Detroit late in the 1980 season.

He spent the first part of that '80 season with Evansville and pitched

Bush Stadium, a.k.a. Perry Stadium and Victory Field, was home to the Indians from 1931 to 1996.

at Bush Stadium on May 30. He lasted six innings, striking out seven and allowing just one run, but did not get the decision. He drew 3,458 fans, however, the largest crowd in two seasons, and they cheered him throughout his time on the mound.

"It's hard to believe the fans are behind me, but I love it," he told newspaper reporters afterward. "It's a feeling you can't express, and that's why you want to give them a great game and make their ride home that much more enjoyable."

Fidrych did a great job cooperating with the media that night. I wanted to show my appreciation, so before the following night's game, I left word that I wanted to see him in my office.

After he sat down in front of my desk I said, "I just want to tell you, I know everywhere you go there are a lot of demands on your time and you go through this day after day after day. On behalf of all of Indianapolis, we really appreciate it how cooperative you were last night. We had a good night with our attendance and that's very important to us, so I just wanted to tell you I'm grateful."

He just stood up, looked at me really hard, moved halfway toward me, leaned in and said, "Thanks for thanking me." And left.

Fidrych pitched twice more at Bush Stadium, on July 6 of that season, when he was credited with a victory, and again on July 3, 1981, when he allowed five hits over five innings and picked up another victory. That appearance didn't help our attendance, though, because he had been a last-minute replacement starter.

He went 6 – 3 for Evansville that season, then pitched two more seasons for Boston's Triple-A franchise in Pawtucket before retiring in 1983 at age 28.

The cause of his demise, the torn rotator cuff, wasn't discovered until 1985. By then, it was too late for him to return to the game, but he left an indelible mark on baseball. Indians fans got to see him both on his way up and his way out, and that's what minor league baseball is about. ●

Howard Kellman's initiative landed him a job with the Indianapolis Indians in 1974.

THE BROADCASTERS

ndianapolis Indians' radio announcer Howard Kellman has broadcast our games every season but two since 1974, a rare record of longevity for the play-by-play voice of any team in any professional sport. Only one other minor league baseball announcer, Jim Weber in Toledo, surpasses him for years of service, and only one announcer in the history of professional baseball has called more championship seasons. Mel Allen broadcast 11 for the Yankees; Howard has worked 8 with the Indians.

Before Howard, though, we had a parade of play-by-play voices pass through the franchise, and even our mere presence on the radio was spotty.

Indians games were first aired on the radio in 1937 when Norm Perry Jr., the son of the franchise's owner, called the games for two seasons. His broadcasts weren't always live, however. The usual practice for home games was that he was on the air from 2:30 to 3:00 p.m., and again from 4:00 to 5:00 p.m. He summarized the action as often as he called it live. For road games, he was given the 4:00 – 5:00 p.m. time slot, during which he recreated action from Western Union wire reports.

He was allowed to call the entirety of Saturday games, but Sunday games were not aired in that "Blue Law" era when most businesses were closed for religious observance.

At least seven other men announced Indians games before Howard took over in 1974, some of them making two tours of duty. Luke Walton was the popular play-by-play voice from 1948 – 55, then left to start his own public relations firm. He returned in 1963, however, in an unusual capacity even for that day.

The Indians could not find a radio station to pay anything to broadcast the games in the championship seasons of 1961 and '62, a source of great frustration for me as the team's new general manager. Radio listeners in that era were beginning to shift their allegiance to various music genres, many of them available on the FM dial.

Walton stepped forward with an offer the following season: he would pay $10 per game to provide limited coverage on a station he had founded, WIGO, which stood for "Indianapolis on the Go."

He was licensed only to broadcast a daytime schedule, however, so he wasn't always able to air games to their completion. Some games he couldn't air at all. But it was better than nothing.

Our daughter Karen was born during Luke's Sunday afternoon broadcast of a game in Rochester, New York. He wasn't there, however. Like all our announcers up until the 1973 season, he did not travel with the team. He took the information off the Western Union wire and recreated it for listeners.

That arrangement lasted just one season, however, and our games were off the air again during the 1964 and '65 seasons. We returned in 1966 on WGEE and have been on the airwaves one place or another ever since.

Carl Grande helped get us back on the air. He was the sports anchor at a local television station, Channel 13. He came to me and said he wanted to broadcast the Indians games on radio. I questioned how he could do both jobs, but he said it would be no problem, he didn't need much time to prepare for his television broadcast because in those days the sports anchor did little more than recite scores. When it came time to leave the game to drive to the television station for his evening broadcast, he'd let one of his backups, either Tom Hession or Johnny

Wade, take over.

Television didn't have much technology in those days, so Grande would pass along scores by writing them on flip cards and holding them over the front edge of his desk while giving sports reports. He might write "Pirates 4, Cincinnati 3" on his cards while talking about something else.

He broadcast our games in 1966 and '67. Through him I met his brother, George, who still helps broadcast the Reds' telecasts on a part-time basis. I have great respect for George because he really works at his craft. He attends spring-training games and sits in 100-degree heat with dust swirling to get to know the players as they advance through the minor leagues.

Three of our announcers went on to land jobs with major-league teams: Bert Wilson (Cubs), Gene Kelly (Phillies), and Jim McIntyre (Reds).

Wilson—whose real name was Ralph Bertam Puckett—broadcast the Indians games in 1941 and '42. He then worked for the Cubs from 1943 – 55, where he gained popularity for catch phrases such as, "I don't care who wins as long as it's the Cubs." He then was hired to broadcast the Cincinnati Reds' television games for the 1956 season, but died of a heart attack in November of '55 at age 44.

Kelly, who worked the Indians games in the 1947 season, broadcast for the Phillies from 1950 – 60, at which time he moved over to the Reds. He's remembered for an innocent gaffe when, toward the end of a Phillies game that went several extra innings and lasted into the early morning hours, said, "That play went five-three if you're scoring in bed."

McIntyre broadcast our games from 1956 – 60, and later worked for the Reds from 1966 – 70. He returned to Indianapolis to become the news director of WFBM television station and handled the play-by-play of Indians games for one more season in 1971.

The Indians' road games were not broadcast live on the radio until 1973, when all of our games were aired on stations in Lebanon and Franklin. Both had weak signals, but between the two of them, we blanketed the Indianapolis area pretty well. Our announcer from that season was not retained, however, so we had an opening heading into the 1974 season.

That's when we hired Howard Kellman, who has been with the Indians ever since except for 1975, when we lost our sponsorship and could not afford to pay him, and 1980, when he pursued other interests.

Howard's story is typical of many broadcasters in that he had to show tremendous initiative and get a little lucky to earn his big break.

Heading into his senior year at Brooklyn College, he sent letters and resumes to all 110 minor-league teams. He received 25 letters back, three from teams that had openings: Spokane, Albuquerque, and Indianapolis.

I was impressed with his initiative and enthusiasm, and wanted to hire a young broadcaster who could grow into the job. I asked Howard to send an example of his work, and he sent a reel-to-reel recording containing his broadcast of one inning of a Yankees-Red Sox game in 1973 from a spare broadcast booth at Yankee Stadium.

I had tapes from about 100 candidates to comb through, so I asked Pat Sullivan, an Indiana state appellate court judge who was on our board of directors, to help me. I didn't ask a front office employee because we only had two other full-timers at the time and they were too busy. Pat and I split up the tapes and we agreed that Howard's was best.

He was enthusiastic, to say the least. When I called to invite him to come out for an interview and asked when he could get to Indianapolis, he said, "How about tomorrow morning?"

That wasn't practical, so we arranged for him to come a few days later. We hired him for the princely sum of $4,000 for the 1974 season. He went back to college to get the final 12 credit hours he needed to graduate following the season, and then returned to Indianapolis in 1976.

We were in danger of losing our broadcast coverage in 1977, however, so I had to send Howard out into the city in February to help find sponsors for the broadcasts. Howard was relatively new to town and didn't have many contacts, so naturally he was hesitant.

"I'm not a salesman, I'm an announcer," he said.

"Well, without a radio station you're not an announcer, either," I replied.

"That's a good point," he said.

Our agreement with the Franklin and Lebanon stations called for us to air 20 one-minute ads per game, eight that we sold to pay the announcer's salary and travel expenses and 12 the stations sold to cover their fee to carry the games.

The Franklin station was on board with us, but prior to the 1977 season, the Lebanon station's general manager Warren Wright called to tell me he had been unable to find sponsors and that we would have to sell additional "spots" and purchase time on his station.

Howard's assignment was to get four sponsors for $2,000 each for the entire season. He beat the pavement for two weeks with no luck. Then one Friday afternoon when he was walking on The Circle downtown, he went into Morrow's Candy Kitchen to get an ice cream cone. He told his plight to the owner, who offered to help but said he couldn't afford to spend $2,000. He was willing to go up to $500, though, which gave Howard the idea of seeking other sponsors for less air time for less money. He quickly rounded up Windsor Jewelers, Joseph's Shoes, and the St. Moritz Steakhouse and we were back on the air.

The moral of the story, Howard likes to say, is that it pays to eat ice cream cones. If not for that fateful visit to the candy store, he likely wouldn't be broadcasting our games today.

He quickly established himself as a successful salesman, and it wasn't long before we added season tickets, special nights, promotions, and other revenue streams to his sales kit. While some of our full-time front office employees balked at sales, Howard set an example for everyone how to go about it.

He has always been a broadcaster first and foremost, however. At the end of the 2018 season, he had called more than 6,000 games for the Indians. ●

Ken Griffey Sr. made a brief return to the Indianapolis Indians in 1974 and fulfilled his promise.

1974

O f all the Indianapolis Indians' teams that didn't win a league championship, the 1974 team probably was the greatest and most deserving. It was stacked. This was the middle of Cincinnati's Big Red Machine era, and we benefited from all the talent the organization had accumulated. Vern Rapp guided the team to the American Association's best record (78 – 57) and was voted the league's Manager of the Year for the second time.

Rapp considered the team the slowest he had managed in his six seasons with the Indians, but thought pitching and defense would compensate for that shortcoming. And they did.

The pitching staff was loaded with future major leaguers. Will McEnaney, Rawly Eastwick, Pat Darcy, Tom Carroll, Pat Zachry, Joaquin Andujar, Santo Alcala, Dick Baney, and Danny Osborn were among those who went on to have at least some success in Cincinnati or with other teams. It finished with the best combined ERA in the league.

Run support was provided by several players who already had major-league experience or were destined to play multiple major-league seasons, such as Ray Knight (13), Dave Revering (5), Roger Freed (8), Doug Flynn (11), Joel Youngblood (14), Junior Kennedy (7), and Ed Armbrister (5).

Tom Spencer's major-league career consisted of just 29 games for the White Sox in 1978, but he was voted the Indians' MVP in 1974 after batting .291 and hitting 14 home runs.

Arturo DeFreites played in 32 major-league games. He was a key player for us that season, but fractured an ankle on May 27 and was lost for the season. He was hitting .316 at the time.

We also lost infielder Junior Kennedy, who was called up by the Reds on August 4. He was hitting .281 and had been named an All-Star.

We also lost Ray Knight for a month. Knight, who was in his second season with the Indians, was a light-hitting (at the time) third baseman, but was an outstanding defender and leader. He suffered a fractured skull when, on July 1, he was hit in the head with a line drive hit by Spencer after volunteering to pitch batting practice before a Monday night game in Des Moines. He returned a month later.

We had enough talent to overcome injuries and call-ups, and the season was filled with success stories. Unfortunately, they didn't add up to a happy ending.

Carroll provided one of the season's highlights when he threw a nine-inning no-hitter on May 24 in Omaha. It remains one of just three in the franchise's modern history, and was the first since Gary Peters did it in 1959.

Baney threw a one-hitter against Oklahoma City at Bush Stadium on June 1. The only hit he allowed was a soft single by Tom McMillan to lead off the sixth inning, which fell just out of reach of a diving Doug Flynn.

A couple of other players made major contributions after being sent down by the Reds temporarily.

Harold "Hal" King was a catcher who had played parts of six seasons with Houston, Atlanta, Texas, and Cincinnati. The Reds sent him to us in July because he had played in only 20 games for them and needed more work.

I assigned him jersey number two. I thought it was a good number for a catcher because the straps of his chest guard wouldn't hide it, but he took it the wrong way.

"I'm no number two," he declared.

That was yet another example of the impact of the racial slights many players had encountered in their careers. Wearing a different number, he played in 60 games for us and hit .256 with 10 home runs before the Reds recalled him in September.

The Reds also sent Ken Griffey Sr. back to us for 43 games. He had played for Indianapolis the previous season, hitting .327, and began the '74 season in Cincinnati. A slow start earned him a return trip to Indianapolis. He didn't waste any time getting to us, either, arriving well ahead of the deadline.

"I wanted to get here as fast as I could because I figure the sooner I get myself together again, the quicker I might get back to the majors," he told newspaper reporters. "I'm back to concentrate on hitting the ball where it is pitched and not try to pull everything like I did with the Reds. And I'll guarantee you one thing. It'll be a different Ken Griffey when I do get back up there."

He fulfilled that promise. He hit .333 for us, then returned to the Reds and never looked back. He went on to play in 19 major-league seasons, was a three-time All-Star and member of two championship teams with the Reds, and still was an effective hitter at the age of 41 when he hit .282 for Seattle. He and his son, Ken Jr., played together for the Mariners toward the end of the 1990 season and again in 1991.

We won 21 of 30 games in July and went on to win the American Association's Eastern Division by 4 1/2 games. We faced Western Division winner Tulsa, managed by former St. Louis Cardinals' All-Star Ken Boyer, in the playoffs. Tulsa's roster also had been diminished by the loss of future All-Star and National League batting champion Keith Hernandez, who had batted .351 for the Oilers before being called up to St. Louis. Catcher Marc Hill, who would play 14 major-league seasons, also had been called up.

Back then, in order to save on travel expenses, the team with the best record played the first three games of championship series on the opponent's field, and then came home for the final four games, if all were necessary.

Tulsa won the first two games on its home field, but we took Game Three. We were feeling good at that point, because we had won seven-of-eight games against the Oilers at home during the regular season.

"My predication still holds," Freed said after the third game. "We'll win three of four in Indianapolis."

We won the next two games to take a 3 – 2 advantage in the series, just one victory from the championship. Game Six, however, brought one of the most agonizing moments in franchise history.

We led 4 – 1 through eight innings as Santo Alcala, our 21-year-old prospect, was breezing along with a two-hitter. The outcome seemed inevitable. Howard Kellman was in his first season as our radio announcer that season, and he and our infielder Lute Barnes had talked before the game about their hopes of being able to utilize the travel arrangements they had made to get out of town early the next day. Kellman wanted to get back to Brooklyn to begin his final semester of college, and Barnes was headed home to the West Coast.

As Barnes stood in the on-deck circle in the bottom of the eighth, he flashed the "OK" sign to Kellman up in his broadcasting booth. Kellman returned the signal. But fate had other plans.

Alcala got the first out. He then gave up a home run to Joe Linsey, but got the second out. We had a two-run lead, and were just one out from winning the championship. But Alcala became anxious in anticipation of the moment and worked too quickly. He walked the next batter on four pitches, then Hector Cruz hit a home run that barely cleared the left field wall to tie the game.

We lost the game in the 15th inning when Tulsa scored four runs after two outs had been made.

It was a crushing defeat, and Alcala took the blame for it.

"Me no concentrate," he said. "Me thinking about the champagne and the celebration."

Tulsa came back the following night to win the championship, 3 – 1, on a three-hitter by Mike Thompson. Zachry threw a seven-hitter for the Indians, but it wasn't enough.

You can imagine the disappointment in our clubhouse. It was the

fourth time in Indians history the team had finished with the best record and failed to win the title, and the fifth time it had happened to
Rapp in his minor-league managing career.

"I guess I'm not supposed to win one of these things," Rapp said.

He was wrong. He won a championship while managing Denver
two years later.

Ray Knight, after suffering his batting practice accident, had said,
"I guess I'm just a born loser."

He was wrong, too. He went on to play in 13 major-league seasons, highlighted by being voted the MVP of the 1986 World Series, in
which he scored the winning run for the Mets. He also was a two-time
All-Star.

Failure is rarely final in baseball, and many of the members of that
team found success in the major leagues. Two of them, Roger Freed
and Dave Revering, would play contrasting roles in a similar story
three years later.

Freed was playing for the St. Louis Cardinals in 1977. A pinch-hitter most of that season, he entered the final game with a .402 batting
average. He could have sat out the final game to preserve that magical
percentage, although he didn't have nearly enough plate appearances
(he finished with 95) for it to count as an official statistic.

The Cardinals trailed 6 – 3 heading into the ninth inning, but rallied. Freed was called upon to bat when they trailed 6 – 4 with two
baserunners. He grounded into a force out to end the game, dropping
his season's average to .398.

Revering, meanwhile, was 24 years old and in his fourth season
with the Indianapolis Indians in 1977. He was voted the team's MVP
for the second consecutive season finishing with a .300 batting average, 29 home runs and 110 RBI. That made him the first Indians player
to appear in more than half of the games and bat .300 since 1973 and
the first to reach 100 RBI since 1962.

He was increasingly frustrated over not having broken into the Majors by that point and was eager to make an impression. He had been
critical of the Reds for not promoting him, and bluntly stated his desire

not to return to them the following season.

"I'm not coming back," he told the *Indianapolis News.* "Not after the way they treated me."

Perhaps he thought preserving a .300 batting average would attract another team. He was just short of it heading into the final game. With the Indians out of the playoff race, he singled in his first at-bat to lift his percentage to that nice round figure then left the game and took a shower. I thought he should have stayed in the game and gone for his 30th home run, which would have been at least as great an accomplishment, but he didn't see it that way.

Revering got his wish the following winter, a trade to Oakland. He played three solid seasons for the A's, then bounced between the Yankees, Blue Jays, and Mariners for the final two seasons of his career. He was with Detroit in spring training in 1983, but failed to make the club. He was offered a minor-league assignment, but refused and retired at age 30.

He had an outstanding career with the Indianapolis Indians, though, and the 1974 season was just the beginning for him. ●

1978

The Indianapolis Indians had a powerful team in 1978, finishing 78 – 57 and winning the Eastern Division of the American Association by a half-game over Evansville. One of the players from that team produced one of the best seasons an Indians player has ever had. John "Champ" Summers, an outfielder, was voted the league's Most Valuable Player and also was recognized as such for all of minor league baseball by Topps and *The Sporting News*. He hit 34 home runs with 124 RBI and batted .368, missing the "Triple Crown" for minor league baseball by .003.

Summers' performance was so outstanding that it overshadowed that of first baseman/outfielder Arturo DeFreites, who "merely" hit .327 with 32 home runs and 102 RBI.

We were lucky to have Summers, because he had been the last player cut by Cincinnati in spring training. Major League Baseball had decided to go with a 24-man roster instead of 25 that season, otherwise he would have stayed with the Reds and played behind George Foster, Cesar Geronimo, and Ken Griffey Sr. in the outfield. But he was better off playing for us every day rather than wasting a season on the Reds' bench. In fact, he later said the season "probably turned my whole life around."

Summers wasn't your typical baseball player. His father had been a boxer, and he was raised to be tough. He had been a parachute trooper during the Vietnam War and was 32 years old by the time he came to us. If anyone deserved the nickname "Champ," he did. He lacked speed on the basepaths and in the outfield, but he brought confidence and toughness to the Indians that season.

He had a sense of humor, too, which helped keep the team loose. During an offday on one road trip during the season, he got into a heated argument with pitcher Doug Capilla. Both of them had major-league experience and were debating whether or not the ball carried well out at Dodger Stadium. Capilla thought it did, Summers thought it did not. The argument became heated and tempers flared, until Summers—who could have broken Capilla in half—said, "The only time the ball carries well at Dodger Stadium is when you're pitching!"

That broke up the room, and ended the argument.

The Indians started slowly that season, falling 12 games behind first-place Evansville on Memorial Day, and were still nine games back with a 51 – 44 record after playing poorly and losing at Denver, 14 – 13, on July 24.

Our play-by-play broadcaster, Howard Kellman, recalls having a beer with manager Roy Majtyka after that game and hearing him say we needed to win 15 of our next 20 games to have a chance to win the pennant.

And wouldn't you know, that's exactly what happened. The Indians defeated Denver the next day, 7 – 6, after getting seventh-inning home runs from DeFreites and Ed Armbrister and went on to win 15 of our next 20 games to build a 66 – 49 record.

We caught up with Evansville on August 10, but our pennant hopes appeared dashed when we lost a 10-inning game to Springfield on August 28 to fall a game behind the Triplets. Two nights later, however, we were a half-game back and clinging to a mathematical chance to complete the comeback with two still to play.

Our game with Springfield (Illinois) got off to a bizarre start because the Bush Stadium field had not been covered the previous night and had been drenched by rain. A helicopter hovered over the field for 30 minutes beforehand to dry it enough for it to be playable.

Our Eastern Division pennant hopes seemed lost when Springfield scored twice in the top of the 10th inning and our first two batters made outs. Trailing by two runs with two outs and having no baserunners wasn't a promising scenario. So Summers retreated to the clubhouse, took off his jersey, and began to drink a beer. But the next three Indians batters—Lynn Jones, Ron Oester, and Harry Spilman—got on base with a single and two walks, so Summers was summoned to put down his beer, put on his jersey, and take his turn at-bat. He proceeded to drive the ball off the top of the right field wall for a bases-loaded triple to score the winning runs.

Some of the fans missed it, because they had given up on the game.

Rex Early, a member of the Indians' board of directors, lived up to his last name by leaving the game before we rallied. He apparently didn't listen to the end on the radio on the way home, either, because the following morning his wife, Barbara, asked how the game had gone as they sat at the breakfast table. Rex began griping about the loss in such a crucial game, but she was reading the morning newspaper at the time and said, "What do you mean? It says here the Indians won!"

He's taken a lot of kidding about that over the years - including from Barbara, who asked with mock suspicion, "Where were you last night?"

Evansville was rained out that same night, but still could win the pennant with a doubleheader sweep on the last day of the season, even if the Indians won. With Summers starring once again by hitting two home runs to lead a 5 – 2 victory over Springfield, we won. We had to wait out the result of the second game of Evansville's doubleheader with Iowa, however. Howard Kellman relayed the play-by-play of the final two innings of the second game over the public address system after our game as the majority of fans remained in their seats and the players listened from the locker room.

Iowa's 3 – 2 victory inspired celebrations all around, especially in the locker room where players doused one another with champagne, beer, and shaving cream.

"This has been a storybook season," Summers said. And it was.

The Indians lost to Omaha, the Western Division winner, in five games in the playoffs, but the season remains one of the most dramatic in franchise history.

Summers was called up to Cincinnati when the season ended and batted .257 in 13 games for the Reds. He played six seasons in the major leagues after that, for four teams, before retiring at age 38.

He also played a central role in one of the most bizarre stories of my career.

In that era, we often took the jerseys from the players after the season and displayed them in the concourse at the stadium the following season. We put them up for sale as well, usually asking $50 for a star player. Champ had been such a major star, however, we asked $75 or $100 for his jersey. Nobody bought it, and on the last day of the season someone broke the glass and stole it.

Several seasons later, Champ was back for an Old-Timer's Day. As he and I were talking, he mentioned he had his former Indians jersey. It turned out that while he was with San Francisco in 1982 and '83 a man had caught his attention during batting practice and told him he had his jersey from his season in Indianapolis. He offered it to Champ, and went to his car to get it. Champ boxed up the jersey and mailed it to me after he returned home.

Just think where that jersey had been. Someone stole it, then gave it or sold it to someone else. It eventually wound up with Champ. He kept it in a drawer for a while and then saw me and gave it back to me.

It's now displayed in the Indians Suite at Victory Field, with a plaque that references his Player of the Year award from *The Sporting News.*

Champ Summers wrote some of the best chapters of the Indianapolis Indians' storybook season in 1978.

George Scherger was described by Pete Rose as "the smartest baseball mind in the world."

1982

G eorge Scherger was hired to manage the Indianapolis Indians in February of 1982. I don't recall the
announcement sending ripples of excitement throughout
the Indians' fan base, but it should have. Anyone who
could have seen past his most recent record and into his
talent and character would have celebrated the news.

Scherger was 61 years old at the time and a veteran of 42 professional seasons as a player, coach, and manager despite losing three
years to military service during World War II. He had never advanced
past the low minor-league levels as a player and had never directed
a major-league team. He had managed 16 different affiliates of the
Dodgers and Reds before coming to the Indians, mostly in baseball
outposts unfamiliar to most people. The previous season he had managed the Reds' Double-A affiliate in Waterbury, Connecticut to a 55
– 83 record.

He had been Sparky Anderson's first manager in the minors, and
Anderson immediately hired him as a coach when Anderson became the
Reds' manager in 1970. Scherger stayed on Anderson's staff through the
Big Red machine seasons until they all were fired in 1978.

"He knows more about baseball than I'll ever know," Anderson
once said.

Pete Rose agreed. When Rose was hired as the Reds' player-manager in 1984, he leaned heavily on Scherger for advice and basically turned the team over to Scherger in the games he played. Some of the Reds, in fact, considered Scherger to be more the manager than Rose. "Most of Sparky Anderson's success here was due to George Scherger, who just happens to be the smartest baseball mind in the world," Rose said then.

It might seem strange someone so highly regarded never got a chance to manage a major-league team, but George didn't strike me as having the charisma and energy for the job at that level by the time I knew him. He was a good, solid baseball man, but didn't have the kind of ego that drove him to want the job. Guys like Vern Rapp desperately want to be a major-league manager, but the George Schergers of the baseball world are content to be coaches or managers in the minor leagues and avoid the pressure of managing a major-league team.

He did a great job for the Indians, though. He declared his goal of winning a championship from the day he was hired, and then went about doing it. He maintained a calm demeanor, but commanded respect and maintained the level of discipline you would expect from someone with a military background. Paul Householder, who played for us in 1980 and '81, had played for George in Nashville in 1979 and recalled Scherger burning Householder's socks in the clubhouse because George didn't like the way he was wearing them.

Householder called George "the best manager I ever played for. He is a no-nonsense man who will get the most out of his players."

George did just that, guiding a team constantly rattled by Reds roster moves to a 75 – 61 record and the championship of the American Association. The call-ups were annoying because the Reds were in the midst of a 61 – 101 season and didn't need our players to help them win meaningful games. We had something to play for, and they didn't.

George won with whomever he was given, though, by remaining flexible and knowing how to bring the best out of the players he had.

"Your material will dictate how you manage," he said.

Outfielder Gary Redus led the offense with a .333 batting average, 24 home runs, 93 RBI, and a league-high 54 stolen bases. Perhaps I get some of the credit for those stolen bases because of my conversation with him during spring training.

The Reds had a patio near the clubhouse of their training site in Tampa where players could get something light to eat for lunch, such as fruit or soup. That setting gave me an opportunity to become acquainted with players new to the Indians, such as Redus.

I was talking with him one day and said, "I noticed you used to steal a lot of bases, but the last couple of years you haven't done it."

"You're right," he said. "I haven't stolen many. I think I'll steal fifty this year."

He went beyond that with 54 stolen bases in what turned out to be his last season in the minors before settling into a 13-season major-league career with the Reds, White Sox, Pirates, and Rangers. He also ran well in his early major-league seasons, peaking at 52 stolen bases with the White Sox in 1987.

We also acquired another valuable outfielder that season, Dallas Williams. He batted .300 and drove in 74 runs. Nick Esasky, a holdover from the previous season, batted .264 and hit 27 homers.

Rookie second baseman Tom Lawless got off to a great start for the Indians, batting .308 through the first 86 games, but became one of the unnecessary call-ups. The Reds were trying to maintain hope among their fans by bringing up some promising young players to give a hint of the future, but I thought Lawless would have been better served if he stayed with us. He could have developed more quickly by playing every day under less pressure.

That's one of the things a minor-league general manager can't control, and it can be frustrating when you have a team with a chance to win a championship. Lawless was, in many ways, the heart and soul of our team that season, but he was just another guy in Cincinnati, where he batted just .212 the rest of the season. He was back with the Indians the following season before reaching the Majors for good in 1984.

Dave Tomlin, who finished with a 9 – 2 record and five saves, led what turned out to be an outstanding pitching staff. He made a league-high 64 appearances despite playing on a bad knee that had to be heavily taped each day he pitched. He never complained, just went out and did his job.

Then there was outfielder Clint Hurdle, who added an interesting dimension to the season. He had been the ninth overall selection in the 1975 draft by the Kansas City Royals. He turned down a chance to play quarterback at the University of Miami in Florida and a scholarship offer from Harvard University to enter professional baseball out of high school. His career started with promise in the Royals' minor-league organization, and he became nationally known when he appeared on the cover of *Sports Illustrated* in 1978. The headline read, "This Year's Phenom."

He played well for the Royals in the playoffs in 1978, '80, and '81, including the World Series in '80 when he had five hits in 12 at-bats. He had been traded to the Reds in December of '81, but hit just .206 in his first 34 at-bats and was sent down to the Indians. It was a difficult time for the former "phenom," and it got worse when he got off to a decent start with the Indians but wasn't called up. He let it affect his attitude for a while, and it got to the point that our fans booed him for lackadaisical effort in the outfield.

Clint Hurdle played for Indianapolis after debuting with the Royals in 1977.

Hurdle wasn't the only slow starter that season. The entire team struggled early on. After one Saturday night loss, Scherger mentioned to Reds farm director Chief Bender that he was going to attend church the next day.

"Oh, you're going to pray for some good hitting, eh?" Bender said.

George seemed offended by the suggestion, and in a serious tone said no, he would never do that.

"What about good pitching?"

Bender asked.

"That's a different story!" George said, smiling.

We eventually got good pitching, but it took a while. We were 4 1/2 games back of Iowa at the end of July and had lost Lawless, but momentum was starting to build with some thrilling finishes. On July 14, in the first game of a doubleheader, we trailed Oklahoma City 13 – 7 heading into the bottom of the final inning. We scored seven runs to win in front of 12,612 fans at Bush Stadium.

On August 6, Bill Scherrer, who had begun the season with Single-A Tampa, pitched a two-hit shutout victory with 12 strikeouts to complete a doubleheader sweep of Evansville in front of more than 11,000 fans.

The next night, Hurdle had seven RBIs in a 10 – 9 victory over Evansville, bringing us back from a 5 – 0 deficit with a double, a grand slam, and a three-run opposite-field homer with two outs in the ninth. We had more than 11,000 fans for that game as well, on AFL-CIO Labor Night.

I was watching the game from the press box and predicted Hurdle's game-winning home run when he went to the plate. As he rounded the bases, I declared to the reporters, "All you guys can live to be one hundred years old and you'll never see a more dramatic home run than that. Of course you're going to have to take better care of yourselves to live to be one hundred."

The Indians still were in third place after Hurdle's heroics, but continued closing fast to beat Iowa by 1 1/2 games in the American Association Eastern Division. We finished our season with two wins over Louisville before nearly 30,000 of their fans, and Evansville helped us clinch the division title by defeating Iowa.

We enjoyed a spirited locker room celebration in the clubhouse in Louisville. That was the occasion in which Hurdle, being Hurdle, suggested to me that the Indians have a "Human's Night" promotion to draw fans. We had been conducting "Ladies Night" for many years, offering reduced or free tickets for women, but those were going out of style. That was his off-beat idea for a replacement.

We went on to defeat Omaha, which was led by our future manager, Joe Sparks, 4 – 2 in the playoffs. With the first three games in Indianapolis, we took a 2 – 1 lead when hard-throwing Freddie Tolliver, who had begun the season in Single-A, threw a two-hitter with 10 strikeouts.

We won Game Four in Omaha, 2 – 1. Mike Dowless allowed one run on three hits through seven innings, and Tomlin picked up the save.

Omaha won Game Five, but we came back to win Game Six, 8 – 0, for our first league championship since 1963 and our first American Association title since '62. Bill Dawley threw a two-hit shutout, Hurdle hit a three-run homer in the fourth inning, and Esasky followed with a three-run blast in the eighth.

That season was what minor league baseball is supposed to be about—a group of players putting aside their major-league ambitions and going after a title by doing all the little things that win games. So many players stepped up to contribute late in the season and in the playoffs. Orlando Isales batted .500 against Omaha and made a game-saving catch while crashing into the wall in Game Four, Redus and Williams each hit .346 in the series, and Neil Fiala came in at .320.

By then, Hurdle was no longer disappointed to be playing with the Indians. He even got serious for a while.

"There's bigger things I've done individually, but this is great because we won it," he said. "And I contributed. I could have rolled over and died after being sent down, but I went out and did the job. This is most satisfying."

I was happiest of all for George Scherger, who was named the Minor League Manager of the Year by The Sporting News. He had done as good a managing job as I've ever seen, getting the most out of a patched-together team and doing it on a shoestring budget. The Reds provided him with no coaches, so he had to take on a lot of added responsibilities, such as pitching batting practice. It was a physically and emotionally demanding season for him.

His strong relationship with the Reds front office paid dividends as well. He was able to talk general manager Dick Wagner out of some of the call-ups Wagner wanted to make, telling him the Reds owed Indianapolis a championship. In all our years together, we had never won a league championship as part of their organization, and George thought it was time.

He also talked Wagner into letting us use the designated hitter in the playoffs, contrary to Wagner's policy, and that eliminated our competitive disadvantage. German Barranca, who had hit .299 in 36 games in the regular season, provided clutch hits in that role.

I'll never forget the postgame celebration in Omaha. George sat quietly in a corner of the visitor's clubhouse, partially undressed, staring at the floor while the players sprayed one another with champagne. Exhausted, he heaved a sigh of relief and said, "I am so happy."

He had set a goal of bringing a championship to Indianapolis and was elated to have done it. But that was enough managing for him. He returned to the Reds as a coach the following season and finished his career in that role, retiring in 1986.

Hurdle knew his time with the Reds was likely over, given all the young outfielders on their roster. He became a free agent after the season and bounced back and forth between Triple A and the Majors for the next five seasons with the Mets and Cardinals. His playing career ended with three game appearances for the Mets in 1987.

He went on to become an outstanding manager; he had the personality for it. He managed Colorado for eight seasons and then took over Pittsburgh in 2010. He was the National League Manager of the Year in 2013 when the Pirates made the playoffs for the first time since 1992.

That brought him back to Indianapolis on occasion. He attended a luncheon in 2013 at which Howard Kellman, our radio broadcaster, interviewed him in front of all the guests. Howard recalled Hurdle's big game in 1982, when he hit the grand slam and game-winning home run in the bottom of the ninth.

"Do you remember that day?" Howard asked.

"Remember it?!" Hurdle said. "The main reason I came here today was to hear you talk about it."

A few years later Hurdle was in Indianapolis for an exhibition game between the Pirates and Reds. We were expecting a full house and my attitude was the same as it had been for those exhibitions with the Reds in the 1970s. We still needed the gate from that game to boost our bottom line. It was a cold and windy day, but the weather wasn't threatening to cancel the game.

Clint took a walk around our park then came back to our clubhouse and said, "Max, I want you to know, if there's one drop of rain we're out of here!" I said, "No you don't, we have fourteen thousand tickets sold. Don't even think about leaving early."

He was joking, of course. But that's the kind of bravado and charisma that helps make him a successful manager. ●

DESIGNATED FOR REASSIGNMENT

The Indians' affiliation with Cincinnati has been like those marriages that are strong for a while, even for several years, but end acrimoniously. We broke loose from the Reds after the 1961 season when they insisted we pay a greater share of player salaries than we could afford, but got back together again in 1968. We enjoyed several good years together after that. We helped develop several players who became key pieces of the Big Red Machine teams. We also won division championships in 1971, '74, and '78, and the league championship in 1982. But I was forced to call the whole thing off again during the 1983 season.

The reason was simple: Reds president Dick Wagner wouldn't let us use a designated hitter. That put us at a competitive disadvantage because all of the other teams in our league were allowed to do so. I had complained about the issue for years, but Wagner wouldn't budge.

He didn't believe it mattered much to the won-lost record whether the pitchers batted or not, and he wanted the pitchers for the Reds' minor-league affiliates to gain experience as hitters because they were going to have to bat if they went on to play for the Reds—or any other National League team. Funny thing was, when the Reds had the opportunity to use a DH in their 1976 World Series sweep of the Yankees, they utilized Dan Driessen in that role. So, it obviously mattered to them then, just like it had mattered to me and the Indians.

I had Cal Burleson research the major-league batting averages of the pitchers who hadn't batted in the minors against the pitchers who had. It turned out to be the reverse of what you might have expected. The guys who had not batted in the minors had better averages in the Majors than those who had taken turns at the plate. I sent the information to Wagner, but he said we had used flawed methodology. He didn't explain, however, and nothing changed.

The issue came to a head in June of the 1983 season. We were just 2 1/2 games behind division-leading Iowa on June 1, and still within reach at 5 1/2 games back on June 28. I sent another appeal to Wagner before our crucial doubleheader at Iowa. We had just signed veteran outfielder Bob Molinaro as a free agent, and he would have been perfect for the DH role. But Wagner rejected the plea once again, and we lost both ends of the doubleheader.

Further complicating matters, Wagner was insisting we sign a new agreement with the Reds covering at least three years. We had operated mostly on one-year agreements until then, with a couple of two-year deals as well. He also imposed a deadline of June 30 for us to sign the new contract he was proposing.

Amid all of this, I had learned Montreal was seeking a new Triple-A affiliate to replace Wichita. So Hank Warren, the Indians' chairman of the board, and I met with Expos president John McHale in Chicago, the site of that season's All-Star game, on July 7. We reached a verbal agreement there and shook hands on it.

Ironically, the Reds fired Wagner four days later. Within 12 hours of that decision, I was notified by Reds executives we could use a DH the rest of that season and in future seasons as well. Those officials tried to convince me to let bygones be bygones and sign a new agreement with them, but it was too late. Although we hadn't signed our contract with the Expos, I felt we still had to honor our verbal agreement with them.

We planned to announce our new affiliation at the end of the season, but word leaked out in Wichita's clubhouse so we made a formal announcement on July 28 when Wichita was in Indianapolis for a series. Naturally, some of our fans were disappointed because they also were fans of the Reds, the major-league team closest to Indianapolis. The complaints were minimal, however, because we explained the situation honestly so that everyone would understand our reasoning. Our most devoted fans had seen the negative impact of not being allowed to use a DH, and were as frustrated by it as we were.

We were forced to make a decision earlier than what we would have liked, but Montreal offered a more desirable working agreement. We just couldn't sit back and hope that everything would turn out well in the fall with the Reds. We had to take advantage of the new opportunity, based on the ultimatum given to us and not knowing that Wagner would soon be replaced.

And thus began one of the most exciting chapters in our history. One that would see the Indianapolis Indians work with Expo front office executives Murray Cook, Bill Stoneman, Dave Dombrowski, and Dan Duquette. Our fans would get to see future major-league stars like Tim Burke, Andres Galarraga, Randy Johnson, Larry Walker, Moises Alou, Mark Gardner, DeLino DeShields, and Marquis Grissom. ●

Max had plenty to smile about during the 1980s.

1984

Our affiliation with the Montreal Expos didn't seem like a natural one for a team in Indianapolis, but it would prove to be the best we had ever had to that point. While the Reds replaced us with Nashville as their Triple-A partner we enjoyed a compatible and successful relationship with the Expos. They always lived up to their business obligations, even in the gray areas, and provided us with excellent talent.

Right away, in fact. We won the American Association pennant in 1984 with a 91 – 63 record. That was a welcome change of pace, as the Reds had provided only one winning team—the 1982 championship team—since 1978.

Our manager that season, and only that season, was Robert "Buck" Rodgers. He had major-league experience, having had a successful run with the Milwaukee Brewers from 1980 – 82, and would go on to lead Montreal for six-plus seasons and then California for more than 300 games. He finished his major-league managerial career with a winning record, and he did an outstanding job for the Indianapolis Indians.

Rodgers had a roster filled with veteran players, at least by minor-league standards, and knew what to do with them. We also were fortunate to have pitcher Joe Hesketh, who made a miraculous comeback from elbow surgery. The left-handed Hesketh had been the number two pick in the 1980 draft by the Expos and was living up to expectations before developing a sore elbow in 1981. Doctors had to take a tendon from his wrist to reconstruct the tendon in his left elbow. He missed the 1981 season and three months in 1982, but worked his way back up through the minors. He very nearly was kept in Montreal that season, but was assigned to the Indians to get in more innings.

Hesketh allowed just two runs in six innings in our home opener. He didn't get the victory, but the Indians did, and he went on to compile a 12 – 3 record for us. He finished the season with the Expos, which turned out to be the start of an 11-season major-league career in which he went 60 – 47.

Another pitcher who fell from the sky had a major impact on our season. Dave Schuler had made a few appearances for the California Angels in 1979 and '80, but had failed to catch on with a major-league team after that and had been released by Kansas City prior to the '84 season.

He was 29 years old, married, a father of a five-year-old daughter, and working as a pitching coach and batting practice hurler for the University of Nebraska at Omaha baseball team when the Indians went to Omaha for a weekend series. He had played for Rodgers at Double-A El Paso in 1977, compiling an 8 – 2 record, so between games of his college team's doubleheader, he drove over to the stadium to seek him out.

"Hey, Buck, do you remember me?!" Schuler shouted from the stands.

Buck did and talked with Schuler. That led to a tryout with the Indians, and we signed him to a contract on May 13. He wound up going 8 – 0 as a relief pitcher and was a vital contributor to our championship. He had a special moment on August 10 when he pitched 2 2/3 shutout innings to clinch a victory over Iowa in the second game of a doubleheader at Bush Stadium with his wife, daughter, parents, two brothers, and extended family all in attendance.

"He goes out and does a job every time," Rodgers said.

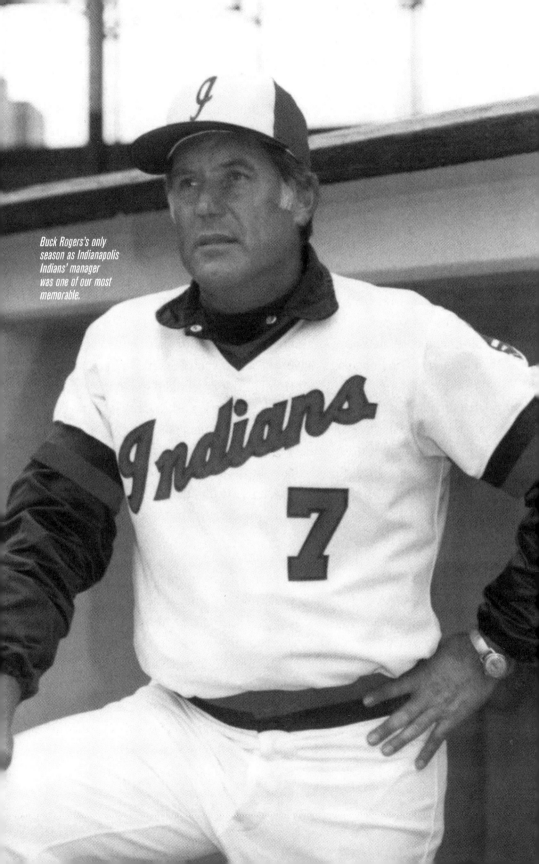

Buck Rogers's only season as Indianapolis Indians' manager was one of our most memorable.

Schuler got one more shot at the Majors, appearing in nine games for Atlanta the following season without a decision, then pitched two more seasons for Triple-A teams before retiring and becoming a minor-league pitching coach.

Pete Rose also dropped in that season as part of the annual exhibition game with our major-league affiliate. Rose had participated in several of them while playing for the Reds, so it seemed odd to see him in an Expos uniform. I always admired the fact he played hard in those games and stayed in the lineup for several innings, unlike some of the other star players who would bat once or twice and then take a quick shower and drive back to Cincinnati.

Rose, 43 years old at the time, was just 152 hits shy of Ty Cobb's all-time record, tied for most games played, and just a month away from returning to Cincinnati as a player-manager when he came to Indianapolis for the exhibition game in '84. He played long enough to bat three times that night. He went hitless, but was the primary reason 7,807 fans showed up for a game that was declared a tie after 11 innings.

The Indians lost to Louisville in the opening playoff round in six games. The Redbirds simply had our number that season, winning 15 of the 22 games between the two teams during the regular season. Louisville went on to defeat Denver in the American Association championship series, 4 – 1.

The postseason disappointment didn't ruin what had been one of the most successful and enjoyable regular seasons in franchise history, however. Buck Rodgers was voted the league's Manager of the Year and the Minor League Manager of the Year by *The Sporting News*. Our shortstop, defensive specialist Rene Gonzalez, won Rookie of the Year honors. Mike Fuentes was great in the clutch with a league-high 13 game-winning hits along with 22 home runs and 80 RBI.

Then there was the player voted the team MVP, a rookie who batted .282, hit 18 home runs, drove in 80 baserunners, and was destined to become the most popular to ever play for the Indians: Razor Shines.

Max celebrates Indianapolis's dramatic 1986 championship with Dallas Williams and Razor Shines.

1986

A fter winning the American Association pennant in our inaugural season with Montreal in 1984, the Indians dropped from first to last in '85, finishing 61 – 81. Felipe Alou was the manager that season. He had come to the Indians with a reputation as a good manager and had done well in other places. He would go on to have success as a major-league manager, such as by winning 100 games with San Francisco in 2003. He also was a terrific guy, and we became good friends. While in Indianapolis, Alou's son Moises, who would go on to a successful major-league career as well, played for Marian College's summer baseball team.

Felipe was not successful with the Indians, though. One of the few bright spots was the emergence of first baseman Andres Galarraga, the Indians MVP who was promoted to Montreal late in the 1985 season. Galarraga would hit 399 home runs and drive in over 1400 runs in his major-league career.

Montreal had sent Buck Rogers to us in 1984 and Alou to us in '85, but their executives accepted my suggestion to hire Joe Sparks in 1986. That was a reflection of the strong relationship between the two front offices at the time. I had accepted their suggestions without complaint the previous two years, and they accepted mine this time.

I admired Sparks because of the job I had seen him do with opposing teams, and was particularly impressed when he managed Iowa in 1978. That was the year the Indians needed Iowa to win at least one game from Evansville in a doubleheader on the final day of the season to win our Eastern Division pennant—the occasion when Howard Kellman relayed the broadcast of the final innings over the public address system at Bush Stadium after we had defeated Springfield.

Iowa was a last-place club in the division that season and could have gone through the motions that night. Furthermore, the White Sox had called up two of its starting pitchers that day. That meant Joe would have to rely on his bullpen to win a game that meant nothing to his team in the standings. But his players fought hard to get a win in the second game, opening the door for us to advance to the playoffs.

He also made a favorable impression on me once when he was managing either Des Moines or Omaha—I don't recall for certain. It was the final game of the season and, again, his team had nothing to play for. It wasn't uncommon in those days for players to turn the hoses on the field overnight and flood it to try to force a cancellation if the final game was meaningless. But Joe was out there raking the field, over and over again, to make it playable. His attitude was you're supposed to play every game whether it means something or not, and he was willing to be a volunteer groundskeeper to make that happen.

Joe came off as arrogant to many people in baseball, giving the impression he thought he knew more about the game than anyone else. But he did know baseball, and he supplemented his tactical knowledge with a steady stream of BS that served him well with his players. The things he said would have sounded ridiculous coming from most people, but Joe could pull it off.

I first witnessed that in spring training of his first season with the Indians. We had a left-handed pitcher, Bob Owchinko, who had pitched 10 seasons in the Majors. He had been bothered by tendinitis in this throwing arm the previous season, and the assumption around baseball was that he was washed-up. He fought hard to stay in the game, though, rehabbing over the winter and sending a video of himself pitching to all the major-league teams. Montreal scout Whitey Lockman watched him throw at a playground near his home in Scottsdale, Arizona, and convinced the Expos to sign him to a contract.

Owchinko showed his determination by approaching Joe and me after dinner one night and saying, "Skip, I'm going to have one helluva year for you this year!"

He no doubt expected Joe to thank him. But that wasn't Joe's style.

"What do you mean you're going to have a helluva year for me?" Joe asked.

"I'm telling you, I'm going to pitch great for you!" Owchinko said.

"I don't want you to have a helluva year," Joe said. "I want you to have a *pretty good* year, and then you won't go to Montreal. We need you here."

Owchinko did just that. He didn't pitch so well the Expos called him up, but he finished with an 11 – 7 record and won eight of his final 10 decisions. He was called up by the Expos after our season and appeared in three games for them, picking up one victory. He retired after that season, but he was an invaluable contributor to what turned out to be one of the most exciting seasons in franchise history.

Part of Joe's ability to create a positive working environment for the players came from constantly selling them on the idea that it was better to be in Indianapolis than in Montreal. That sounds crazy now, but that was the salesman side of him, and it worked. The fact the Indians were contending for a championship in 1987 and the Expos were struggling through a losing season gave him all the ammunition he needed.

He once called Owchinko into his office after a couple of strong performances and issued a warning with mock seriousness.

"That's not going to happen again," he said. "When I put you out there, I don't want you pitching shutouts, or you're going to fool around and get yourself called up to Montreal."

Another day, I was taking care of paperwork for Herm Winningham, who had been called up by Montreal, while Joe sat in my office.

When Herm came by to get his travel arrangements, Joe said in all seriousness, "OK, you're going back to Montreal, son. But I just want you to know, if you do well there we'll bring you back to Indianapolis!"

Herm was like, "Oh, yeah, yeah, Skip, I know! I'll do it!" He was so used to saying, "Sure, Skip, whatever you say …" that he bought into the idea.

Joe just had a knack for communicating with the players. He might have rubbed some management people the wrong way, but he and I got along well and his line of BS worked with the guys on the field. He was always finding ways to motivate them. He'd say things like, "You know what Joe Blow over there said about us?" He might take a quote he had seen in the newspaper and exaggerate it to make it sound worse than it was to make the players angry. He just knew how to twist things to the team's advantage.

The Indians finished 80 – 62 that season, the best record in the American Association. The roster changed frequently as the Expos scrambled to field a winning team, but Sparks maintained a spirited atmosphere. Razor Shines's return on July 4 was a major boost as well.

The season came down to a Game Seven matchup with Denver, which had won the Western Division title in the regular season. It held a 4 – 2 lead going into the bottom of the ninth inning of the game at Bush Stadium, but the Indians put together what might be the most historic rally in franchise history.

Darrell Baker, who batted .284 in the regular season, led off with a crisp single to center. Rene Gonzales, a .273 hitter, hit a high infield chopper that advanced Baker and brought the first out. Tom Nieto's single to right advanced Baker to third base, and Tom Romano singled to score Baker and move Nieto's pinch-runner, Nelson Norman, to second.

Rob Dibble, who was destined to accomplish great things in the Majors, took over on the mound at that point, but Casey Candaele greeted him with a sharp single to right. Norman, however, got caught in a rundown between third and home and committed the second out.

Romano moved to third and Candaele to second during the rundown, and that brought Razor Shines to the plate. It was a moment

Billy Moore contributed one of the biggest hits in Indianapolis Indians' history.

made for a movie, as one of the greatest clutch hitters in franchise history squared off against a future two-time major-league All-Star with a championship on the line.

Denver, though, employed the traditional strategy of walking Razor to load the bases with two outs. Dibble's first lobbed pitch well outside the strike zone revealed the plan. Razor was so incensed by not having the opportunity to make history that he slammed his bat on home plate and broke the bat.

The umpire told Razor he couldn't stand in the batter's box with a broken bat even if he was going to be walked, so he had to go to the dugout to get a new one. Billy Moore, the batter on deck, was irritated by the delay. He knew then he was going to hit and didn't want to stand there so long. Razor was jumping around in the box, trying to bait Dibble into pitching to him or perhaps balking, but it didn't work. On his way to first base, he turned to Billy and yelled, "Win this thing, right here and now!"

When Razor reached first base, Denver's Lloyd McClendon—who would go on to play eight major-league seasons and manage both Pittsburgh and Seattle—couldn't believe what he had just seen. "Razor, are you crazy?!" he said. Razor replied, "Lloyd, if Billy Moore doesn't get a hit here and you guys celebrate on my field, you'll see how crazy I am."

Moore, who led the team with 23 home runs during the regular season, composed himself and got the hit that kept Razor sane off a two-strike pitch. The hit flew into left field and scored Candaele for the winning run. Many of the 3,254 fans rushed onto the field to join the celebration as Candaele ran into a sea of celebrating teammates at home plate.

"It was like all of Indianapolis was out there," Candaele said later. "For a moment, it almost seemed like time stood still."

That game helped make up for all the times we won regular-season titles but couldn't get it done in the playoffs. You usually need breaks to win championships, and we had caught one that season when Cincinnati called up Barry Larkin from Denver's roster during the regular season. Larkin, who would go on to be selected to play in 12 major-league All-Star games, was hitting .329 for Denver before the promotion, so we really benefited from his absence.

The Game Seven victory remains the most exciting Indians game I've witnessed in more than 60 years with the organization, and the locker room celebration was wild. Two of our major-league veteran pitchers, Len Barker and Larry Sorensen, sat in a corner and smoked cigars and watched quietly, but the rest of us cut loose. Personally, I stripped down to swim trunks and a T-shirt and danced on equipment trunks with Razor and outfielder Dallas Williams, who had hit .289 during the regular season.

Sparks was selected Minor League Manager of the Year by The Sporting News that season, and deservedly so. He got the absolute most out of his players despite all the turnover that resulted from Montreal's roster moves. In the locker room afterward, he said something like, "I can't tell you how much I had to think while filling out the line-up card every day to get all of you outfielders playing time."

One of those outfielders shouted out, "But you did a helluva job, Skip!"

And he did.

Joe remembers sending his coach, Jerry Manuel, up to my office before the game to get the device used to measure for championship rings as a motivational ploy to inject more confidence into the team. I recall doing it on my own. Razor Shines would tell you it didn't matter, that the players knew they were going to win.

Regardless, I had everyone's ring size in hand when the game ended. Thanks to Billy Moore, I needed them. ●

Joe Sparks directed the Indianapolis Indians to three consecutive championships from 1986-88.

1987

I t was going to be impossible to match the drama of the 1986 season when the Indianapolis Indians reported for spring training the following year. But we came close. With just seven players returning, we still managed to win another championship despite finishing third in the American Association with a 74 – 64 record, four games back of first-place Denver. It was a drama-filled season from beginning to end, full of great individual stories.

The American Association switched from two four-team divisions to one eight-team league before the season began. I was against the change but was outvoted 7 – 1, an occurrence that wasn't all that unusual.

We opened the season on the road and went 5 – 2, but Joe Sparks didn't come home with the team. He had to stay in a hospital in Denver with Meniere's disease, an inner ear disorder that causes vertigo. Jerry Manuel took over and went 6 – 1, but the only loss came at an unfortunate time: a 15 – 6 defeat in our home opener to Oklahoma City before 11,469 fans.

Two pitchers who had found success in the major leagues were part of our fast start.

Dennis Martinez was 32 years old when the '87 season began. He had won 102 games over 10 seasons for Baltimore, but wore out his welcome because of alcohol issues. He had finished the '86 season with Montreal, going 3 – 6, but didn't receive the interest in free agency he desired and re-signed with the Expos in May. They sent him to Indianapolis to give him a chance to redeem himself.

"I just have to remember what alcohol did to my life," he said upon joining the Indians. "It almost destroyed my life, my career and my family."

Martinez started the season 1 – 2 with an 8.10 ERA, but then threw a one-hitter with no walks for a win against Buffalo. He won his next two games as well, and was 4 – 3 when the Expos recalled him. He went 11 – 4 for them the rest of that season and pitched 11 more seasons before retiring in 1998 at age 44 with a 245 – 193 career record.

Pascual Pérez was an even better story.

Standing 6-foot-3 and weighing just 160 pounds, he came to the Indians with a reputation for having a bad arm, a bad attitude, and a drug problem. He had gone 15 – 8 and 14 – 8 for Atlanta in the 1983 and '84 seasons, but declined to 1 – 13 in '86. The Braves released him after that season, and he played winter baseball in the Dominican Republic before joining Indianapolis.

He had become nationally infamous shortly after joining the Braves in August of 1982 when he got lost on the I-285 loop that circles Atlanta. Unfamiliar with his environs, he missed his exit and drove the 64-mile lap around the city. He missed it a second time as well, and, some say, a third time, too.

He missed his start that day but won a place in the hearts of fans who had struggled to navigate the city's traffic. His comical mishap also loosened the Braves' clubhouse, and they went on a winning streak that propelled them to the playoffs.

The strange thing is, he showed an uncanny sense of direction while in Indianapolis.

He was back with the Indians briefly the following season, in 1988. I picked him up at the airport and headed for the motel at the Indianapolis Motor Speedway, where our players stayed before they found an apartment. Traffic was backed up when we neared the motel, however, due to a long line of motorcycles waiting to enter the speedway and take a lap around the track.

I needed to take him to the ballpark first and then back to the motel and he told me exactly how to go about it to avoid all the traffic. I can't speak for what happened in Atlanta, but his sense of direction in Indianapolis was excellent.

He had no problems finding his way to the stadium in 1987, either. Like Martinez, his season started poorly. He gave up three earned runs in 2 1/3 innings in his first start against Louisville on May 13 and was kicked out of the game for profanely arguing—in Spanish—a balk call in the second inning.

He bounced back with a 6 – 0 record and 1.4 ERA in June to lead a month-long rally in which the Indians went 20 – 9.

We moved into first place on June 14 and were up four games by the end of month despite having started 26 – 21 and falling to fourth place in the American Association standings earlier in the season.

We were holding onto a one-game lead in August when we had to go on a 15-day road trip. Indianapolis was hosting the Pan American Games that summer, and Bush Stadium was needed for the baseball competition. We had a scary moment when the US team played Cuba. CBS was televising the game nationally, and their announcers mentioned reports that a bomb had been planted in the stadium. The broadcast later was knocked off the air by an electrical storm, which for a few moments made television viewers wonder if something terrible had happened. However, the game went off without a problem after a delay to dry the field.

The Indians went 7 – 5 on the trip and returned with a 1 1/2-game lead over Louisville. With our final 12 games at home, it appeared we were set up for a strong finish, but it didn't turn out that way. The first of those 12 games lasted 19 innings and took 5 hours, 40 minutes to complete. It tied the record for the longest game played at Bush Stadium, which had been set in 1985.

Not only that, Razor Shines was injured and wasn't playing. Not only that, the Expos were battling to win the National League East and had injured players to replace, so they called up four of our better performers: first baseman Jack Daugherty and infielder Luis Rivera, both of whom were All-Stars that season; as well as outfielder Tom Romano and relief pitcher Randy St. Claire.

We were two games back of Louisville heading into a three-game series that closed the season. We lost the first two games to slip to fourth place in the standings, but got a lift by winning the final game. Billy Moore, hero of the '86 championship series, had fractured his collarbone in May after running into the outfield wall in Omaha. He came back from a six-week absence to hit a two-run single in the eighth inning for that victory.

The Indians eliminated Louisville in the first round of the playoffs, then faced Denver again for the league championship. It was a difficult turnaround, as the team arrived back in Indianapolis after midnight following the final game with Louisville and had to be back at Bush Stadium at 5:00 a.m. to catch the shuttle to the airport for the flight to Denver. Needless to say, the players were in no condition to be at their best in Game One that night in Denver and lost, 2 – 1.

"I guess we forgot to leave a wakeup call," Sparks said.

The Indians won the next two games, however. Razor Shines, back from his injury, hit a home run, and Ron Shepherd hit two in Game Three, sending us home with a 2 – 1 lead.

Charlie Lea was scheduled to start Game Four at Bush Stadium, but was called up by Montreal that morning. Lary Sorensen, by then a 31-year-old veteran who had won 18 games for Milwaukee nine years earlier and been part of our championship team the previous season, took his place and allowed just one run on five hits in 8 1/3 innings with no walks and eight strikeouts.

We won the championship the following night with a 10 – 5 victory. Razor broke open the game with a two-run single for his seventh RBI in 10 playoff games, and Ron Shepherd finished it off with a solo home run over the left field wall. Shepherd, who had been one of Toronto's final cuts in the spring and claimed on waivers by the Expos, batted .483 in the playoffs and was voted MVP.

Tim Barrett, who finished the season with a 10 – 1 record, got the victory. Kurt Kepshire, a member of the Indians' 1982 championship team, pitched the final 1 1/3 innings and allowed no hits to get the save.

It was that kind of season. We had to apply Band-Aids to the roster all season, but people just kept coming through for us. That team had great depth, and great character as well.

One of the players I was really happy for was infielder Nelson Norman. He was 29 years old by then and had been knocking around the minor leagues for the previous five seasons. He had the best season of his career that year, batting .292 in the regular season and .314 in the playoffs.

"This means more to me than anyone can imagine," he said after the final game. "In the ninth inning there were tears in my eyes. It was so bad I didn't want a groundball hit to me because I couldn't see. I couldn't help it. I was so excited. Then I looked over at Johnny [Paredes], and he was crying, too.

"This is my first ring, and I'll wear it every day." ●

Indianapolis's 1987 championship was one of the highlights of Nelson Norman's career.

Randy Johnson was an intimidating pitcher for the Indianapolis Indians—even for mannequins.

1988

R andy Johnson is one of the greatest players ever to
wear an Indianapolis Indians uniform, but not because of what he did while playing for the Indians.
The intimidating 6-foot-10, hard-throwing lefthander
ranks as one of the best pitchers in history, a five-time
Cy Young Award winner and 10-time All-Star who ranks
second all-time in strikeouts (4,875). We had him in the
1988 and '89 seasons when he was a 24- and 25-year-old
prospect in Montreal's system. Predictably wild, he had
a combined 9 – 8 record and an average ERA of 3.08 in
those two seasons, with 81 walks and 128 strikeouts in
131 1/3 innings.

He was raw but full of promise, and he took a major step forward
in his Hall of Fame career with us.

One of my lasting memories of him is from a preseason team luncheon with Mayor William Hudnut in the City-County Building, an
annual event in that era. One of the Mayor's secretaries was Sandy Allen, who, at 7-foot-7, was the tallest woman in the world. Randy, who
could empathize with an unusually tall person, was fascinated with her
and spent the hour talking with her in the outer office. He might have

had food brought out to him, I don't recall, but he was far more interested in her than in the Mayor's remarks or eating lunch.

Randy normally wasn't sociable, and in fact could be downright surly at times. He had a temper, too, but our manager Joe Sparks, and our pitching coach Joe Kerrigan, worked with him diligently and patiently to extract his vast potential. Sparks was the taskmaster who pushed Randy to be more disciplined on his offdays while Kerrigan worked on the details of pitching, such as how to hold runners on base.

Randy got off to a good start in his first season with the Indians. By June 15 he was 6 – 4 and had won five straight outings with a 1.18 ERA during that stretch. He was to start against Richmond that day and had been informed beforehand he would be called up to Montreal afterward if all went well. A few Expos executives were on hand to see their hot prospect first-hand.

Johnson got off to a good start in the game, but with two outs in the third inning, Jeff Blauser hit a line drive that ricocheted off his left hand. Johnson fell to the ground as a hush fell over the park. He was helped up and taken out of the game to get X-rays, but on his way to the locker room, he grabbed his jacket on the bench and, in one fell swoop, smacked the bat rack with his right hand. It turned out his pitching hand was fine, with nothing more than a cut, but he broke a bone on the outer portion of his right hand because of his temper tantrum.

"I am not saying what he did was right, but this will teach him a painful lesson," Kerrigan said after the game.

It wasn't long before Randy's left hand recovered well enough for him to throw simulated games while he waited for the right hand to finish healing. Only problem was, we couldn't find anyone to stand in the left-handed batter's box against him. Sparks made a call to my son, Bruce, who at the time was the director of special projects. Joe wanted a mannequin to replace a human being after the team returned home, and that certainly qualified as a special project.

Bruce was able to obtain one from Indianapolis' world-renowned Children's Museum, although technically it was a woman-equin. We put "her" in a uniform, including a batting helmet and eye black, and taped a bat to her shoulder.

Randy was to pitch to her every fifth day as part of his rehabilitation. But he still had control problems, and gradually began taking chunks out of her.

Johnson, though, came back to pitch one of the most important games of his career after he recovered. Facing International League-champion Rochester in the Triple-A Classic, the Indians dropped the first two games on the road. Starting Game Three in Rochester, Johnson went the distance for the first time in two years and allowed just two runs and eight hits with eight strikeouts.

The Indians returned home to win the next three games and capture the championship.

Six days after his Game Three victory, Johnson made his major-league debut for Montreal and was credited with the win after pitching five innings against Pittsburgh and allowing two runs. He pitched a complete game in his next start against the Cubs, allowing one run and striking out 11 at Wrigley Field, and finished the season with a 3 – 0 record for the Expos.

Randy pitched in three games for the Indians in 1989, going 1 – 1 with a 2.00 ERA, but he went 0 – 4 with a 6.67 ERA after the Expos called him up. They gave up on him—too soon, obviously—and traded him to Seattle, where he became an All-Star and threw his first no-hitter in 1990.

Sparks was ready to move on after the 1988 season as well. While we all were celebrating our championship in the clubhouse after the Game Six clincher, he called a few front office executives and board members into his office and dropped a bomb.

"I think this will be it for me here," he said. "I think it's time to move on."

I asked, "Why not come back and win it again?"

"I'm afraid I'll screw it up," Joe said.

He was kidding. He was anxious to get to the Majors and already had arranged to become a hitting coach in Montreal. He believed in the theory that a coach or manager wears out his welcome with the players after a few seasons and needs to move on before they tune him out.

He coached for the Expos in 1989, then took a gamble by joining Bucky Dent's staff in New York in 1990 as the bench coach. Joe had been Dent's manager for a Class-A team in the White Sox organization, and the two were close. But Dent, who had taken over the Yankees late in the '89 season, was fired on June 6, 1990 after his team started 18 – 31. Dent's coaching staff was let go as well in one of Yankee owner George Steinbrenner's classic purges. Not only was Sparks out of work, former Indians outfielder Champ Summers, who was Dent's hitting coach, was gone as well.

It's traditional in baseball for someone let go during the season to continue receiving his paycheck as scheduled until his contract expires. The Yankees, though, paid off everyone with one check. They seemed to want the slate cleared as quickly as possible so they could start over fresh with a new manager and coaches.

Joe returned to managing by taking over Toledo's International League team, then worked as an advance scout for St. Louis and Oak-

Joe Sparks, foreground, charged out of the dugout to celebrate our 1988 championship.

land before retiring in 2008.

Perhaps if he had stayed in Montreal instead of going to New York he would have gotten a shot as a major-league manager. We'll never know how that would have gone for him, but there's no doubt he was great for the Indianapolis Indians. ●

SPRING TRAINING

S pring training was always an exciting time of the year for me. Just about the time you've had enough of the Midwest winter, you fly into the warm embrace of the sunshine in Florida or Arizona and begin watching baseball again. The crack of wooden bats and the pop of horsehide (or, after 1974, cowhide) balls smacking leather mitts made for one of the greatest melodies I've ever heard. For a Triple-A general manager, every season is an adventure because the roster turns over so drastically from year to year. And, if you happen to have changed affiliates that year, it turns over completely, with a new manager and an entirely new group of players. It's always interesting to experience the fresh beginning that arrives each spring, and to look for reasons to be optimistic.

It's not as enjoyable as it once was, though.

Major-league teams now treat minor-league exhibition games as laboratories rather than legitimate contests. They might have a hot young prospect bat in the leadoff position in every inning to get a better look at him, or to try to accelerate his development. Or, if a pitcher gets in trouble and can't get the side out, they just call the inning to a halt and move on.

I remember the occasion when an opposing pitcher gave up several hits and runs in a game. Finally, the manager of his team called off the inning, claiming the pitch limit had been reached, and we changed sides. The same pitcher took the mound again in the next inning, however. I complained, reminding them they had said he had reached his pitch limit, but they said, "That was for that inning, not for the game."

Anything goes today. If somebody in leadership on a major-league team wants Joe Blow to get more at-bats, they'll send him over to the Triple-A affiliate and have him lead off every inning. A team might even put a guy on first base, whether he had attained the base or not, just to see if he can steal.

It's player development gone amuck, I believe. I have too much respect for the game to see it corrupted like that, even in spring training. Winning and losing is still important, and I like to see who can deliver in clutch moments. There are none when the game isn't treated seriously.

This twisted approach began in the 1980s, and has only grown from there. It eventually became impossible to keep score of the games. The *Star* and *News* sent reporters to our spring-training site for years, but when that ended I would call in information from the game to the Indians publicity director and he would fan it out to the media. It became more and more difficult for me to keep a coherent scorebook when players were batting in every inning or pitchers were coming and going at the whim of the manager. Eventually, I had to give up.

Major-league affiliates today also need or want more time to evaluate their players, so they delay sending players to the Triple-A teams until just a few days before the season begins. That's unfortunate, because it becomes difficult to generate interest back home. You need a familiar name from the previous season or a prospect who has received a lot of publicity to offer something worth writing or talking about in your local media.

This practice also prevents minor-league teams from bonding as well as they once did in spring training. Not only do the players spend less time together in a relaxed setting, their managers and coaches are delayed in the transfer from the major-league team to the minor-league affiliate they'll be leading in the regular season.

Although I enjoyed spring training, one of my earliest memories of it is an unpleasant one. In the early 1960s, when we were affiliated with the White Sox and training in Florida, the black and Latin players were made to stay in motels outside of town. This was about 15 years after Jackie Robinson had broken the color barrier, but we were still dealing with discrimination in the South.

A van would go out to pick them up each morning and bring them to practice. Our front office personnel and coaches called it the "Blueberry Run," because of the darker skin tone of the players. That was shocking to me. I hadn't grown up in the South, so I hadn't experienced that sort of blatant prejudice.

The affected players, though, accepted the situation without complaint. That simply was the way things were done in those times. Fortunately, the times were changing. ●

No player brought more joyous moments to the Indianapolis Indians than Razor Shines.

R-R-R-R-R-R-R-R-R-AZOR SHINES

A fter we signed our working agreement with the Expos in the summer of 1983, Montreal's farm director Bob Gebhard made a promise to me.. ● "You're going to have a player on your team next year who, I guarantee you, within the first two weeks of the season, will be your most popular player," he said.

He was right. That player was Anthony Ray Shines, a first baseman who was an 18th-round draft pick of the Expos' in 1978 and had been working his way up through their minor-league system. He was 27 years old by the time he got to us. His major-league experience consisted of just three games with the Expos at the end of the 1983 season after playing for their Double-A affiliate in Memphis and their Triple-A affiliate in Wichita.

While many players with that kind of résumé are nearing the end of their baseball career, his in many ways was just beginning.

His nickname was Razor, passed down from his grandfather and father. "Razor" had been their actual middle name, and he later passed it on as a middle name for his son and grandson. It no doubt fed into his popularity with the fans, many of whom probably didn't even know his first name.

Although he was our Most Valuable Player in 1984, his esteem grew from more than stats. The fans loved him for his aggressive style of play and infectious enthusiasm. If the Indians were behind but beginning to mount a rally, he'd be hollering to the other dugout, "Here we come! Here we come!"

He was cocky, yes, but he could back it up. He might not impress you if you watched him during the early innings, but if he was at bat with a tying run on base late in the game, he would usually produce. To this day, he's one of the best clutch hitters in Indians history. Our radio broadcaster, Howard Kellman, believes it was because he had a knack for relaxing in clutch moments. He might swing for the fences early in the game, but he stayed calm and settled for a base hit when it was needed late in a close game.

He engaged the fans as well, signing autographs and shaking hands before games and waving to them when they called his name during the game. He further enhanced his popularity by living in Indianapolis in the offseasons toward the end of his nine-year run with the Indians.

Without a doubt, part of his popularity came from the creative manner in which our public address announcer Kurt Hunt introduced him when he came to bat. One night when we had a small crowd for a game in 1984, Kurt impulsively tried to liven things up by drawing out Razor's nickname in a deep, guttural tone, proclaiming "R-r-r-r-r-r-r-r-razor Shines!" If you remember the television commercials for Sugar Frosted Flakes that featured Tony the Tiger declaring "They're gr-r-r-r-r-r-r-eat!" you get the idea.

Razor was taken aback and shot a quizzical glance over his shoulder up toward the public address announcer's booth the first time Kurt tried the introduction. But he hit a double, so Kurt repeated it the next time. Razor got another hit, and the introduction stuck for the rest of his career with the Indians. He grew to love it, and felt it gave him adrenaline.

The fans always responded enthusiastically, either by cheering or mimicking Kurt. Some of them even called out "R-r-r-r-r-azor Shines!" when they saw him out in public. It became such a legendary part of Indians history that, more than 30 years later, a friend's wife asked Kurt to record a similar intro for use on her cellphone voice mail greeting.

After his MVP season with us in '84, Razor was promoted to the Expos' roster as part of the September call-up. He appeared in 12 games and got six hits in 20 at-bats, providing a glimmer of hope for a major-league career. He began the 1985 season with Montreal as well, but was sent back to us on May 18 after playing in just 14 games. I told the Expos if they weren't going to play him, we would be happy to have him back, and they agreed.

Most players would have been disappointed, and some would have moped around and taken as much time out of the 72-hour grace period as they could before arriving. Not Razor. He caught the first flight out of Montreal and arrived in time to play for the Indians that evening.

Razor Shines, shown with The Famous Chicken and a fan, always had time to meet the public.

"I love baseball, and that was my job to get here and play," he told newspaper reporters. "I'm just glad to get the opportunity to play."

He hit a three-run homer that night in a loss, and went on to ignite a rally that took the Indians to within three games of the lead. After he was called back up to the Expos on July 22, however, we collapsed and finished last in our division, 20 games below .500. We were 33 – 33 in the games he was in uniform for us, but 28 – 48 without him. His .308 batting average was only part of the reason for the difference. We missed his spirit, too.

That 1985 season ended fatefully for Razor in Montreal. He was sent into the final game of the season at Shea Stadium in New York as a pinch-runner. It was a curious move by Buck Rogers, who had moved up to manage the Expos that season, because the one thing Razor couldn't do was run fast. He barreled into second base to try to break up a double play, but Mets second baseman Wally Backman dodged his slide and Razor tore cartilage in his right knee when he collided with the bag and had to undergo surgery.

Razor hit just .120 in 47 games with the Expos, although he did break up Dennis Eckersley's late no-hit bid with a single in one game. Such is the difference between the pitching in Triple A and the major leagues. Some players can star at one level but not quite cut it at the next level, and Razor was one of them.

He was perfect for the Indians, however, with his persona and clutch-hitting ability. He was built like an NFL linebacker, standing 6-foot-1 and 210 pounds, and often played like one. He was a blue-collar guy who always played hard and injected energy and confidence into his teammates. He had a distinctive lumbering home-run trot in which he would pause and step around each base along the way.

He was versatile, too. He was primarily a first baseman and designated hitter, but played third base and catcher as well. He even made brief appearances as a pitcher a couple of times for the Indians and once for the Expos—successful ones, at that, as he allowed no earned runs in four total innings for the two teams.

I once congratulated him for performing so well as an emergency pitcher, but made the observation he only threw fastballs. His response: "I have a heck of a slider, too, but I haven't needed it yet."

Like I said, he was confident.

Razor's knee injury at the end of the 1985 season proved to be a major setback, in more ways than one. He rehabilitated over the winter, but didn't have a contract for the next season. He refused to report to spring training because he knew he couldn't earn a roster spot with a weak knee. That nearly ruined his relationship with the Expos because they did not feel he had communicated well with them during the off-season and perhaps questioned his physical condition.

Without Razor, we quickly established ourselves as a title contender in the 1986 season. And then, without warning, he came walking into my office on July 4 and announced he was ready to play. I called Bob Gebhard to tell him I wanted to sign him because we were in a pennant race and needed his bat and charisma. I also told our first-year manager, Joe Sparks, of my intention. Sparks had no personal involvement with Razor, so he was ambivalent.

I told Razor I would sign him, but with some conditions. I had been an advocate for him since his arrival in Indianapolis, but the Expos had become skeptical because of his holdout. I told him I would only sign him to a two-year contract, which is rare in the minors where one-year deals are the norm. I also told him we didn't have a roster spot for him and he would have to start out as a bullpen catcher. In fact, we had another player waiting for a roster spot to open so Razor would be one spot removed from becoming an active player. He said OK to everything, because he was anxious to play ball again.

"I'm eager to go out and prove to people that Razor Shines can still play this game," he told newspaper reporters after signing. "I consider myself married to baseball. I love it more than I can express. And I've missed it more than I can express."

Sparks remained skeptical as the season played on and our former MVP was killing time as a bullpen catcher—a catcher with a bad knee who couldn't even crouch into the proper position. One day Joe even asked me, "What did you get me into here, Max?"

The breakthrough came on July 25, when the Indians were playing in Des Moines. I was in Cincinnati entertaining a group of our season ticket-holders when I took a call from Sparks, who said we needed to add a catcher because the Expos had just recalled our starter, Tom Nieto. I said we could activate Razor because he had broken into the minor leagues at that position.

Razor didn't wait long to win over Sparks. He hit a pinch-hit double off the right field wall in the 11th inning to ignite a game-winning rally in his season debut. He provided another game-winning hit the next day with a seventh-inning single. He added a third game-winning hit, an eighth-inning home run, on August 6, and had a fifth by August 15.

He also caught one or two of those games and wowed Sparks with his toughness. His surgically repaired right knee still bothered him, so he put his left knee on the ground and crouched at the waist while catching. It looked strange, but he had no choice; he could barely stand up at the time. And he got the job done.

Razor understandably became frustrated as he continued to turn in productive seasons for the Indians without getting a call-up from the Expos. He played six games for them at the end of 1987 season, but by 1989, it had become obvious he was running out of major-league opportunities.

He hit .305 for us in the 1988 championship season. The following winter, the Pittsburgh Pirates offered him a contract and promised him a fair opportunity to make their roster. A lot of major-league teams do that, holding out that carrot to bolster their talent pool for spring training and their minor-league affiliates.

The catch was, they weren't offering him a *guaranteed* major-league contract. They told him they didn't have enough room on their roster for that, and could only offer a Triple-A contract.

He came by my office that winter to talk about it, and I tried to be honest with him.

"Once you sign that contract, they can do anything they want with you," I said. "They can send you to Timbuktu. Don't believe everything you hear. You started in Indianapolis, and we love you here. I want you to play in the Majors, but don't fall for this line that you'll have a chance to play for Pittsburgh."

He thought it over for a while, but eventually came back one day to tell me he was going to sign with the Pirates, taking a final shot at the Majors at age 33.

I said, "Razor, I have two questions: Do you believe them when they say you'll have every opportunity to make their team?" He said he believed them. I said, "Here's my other question: Do you believe when they break camp you can be one of their best twenty-five players?" He said yes.

I stood up, walked over, gave him a big hug and said, "Razor, go sign that contract."

His dream didn't pan out. Major League Baseball's 32-day lockout cancelled most of spring training in 1990, dampening his opportunity to win a spot on the Pirates' major-league roster. I later heard that they never planned to keep him, anyway. He began the season in Buffalo, but was sent to Mexico City of the Mexican League after a couple of weeks. He was leading the league in batting and was second in home runs, but things were such a mess there that the club didn't even tell him when he was called back to the Pirates' Triple-A franchise in Buffalo in August. His agent called to ask him why he hadn't reported, but he knew nothing about it. He caught a bus back to Mexico City that night and then found transportation to Buffalo without saying a word to anyone.

He batted just .170 in 42 games with Buffalo. He returned to Indianapolis for the 1991 season after signing a new contract at the age of 34. Clearly, he and the Indians needed one another. He had been miserable playing in Buffalo and Mexico City, and the Indians had finished last without him.

He played the final three seasons of his career with us. He retired after the 1993 season, when he was a part-time player and coach and even filled in as the manager for two games in June when Marc Bombard was not available. He was good to the very end, playing in 65

games at age 36 and batting .276. He finished strong, too, with a batting average about .375 over his final 12 games.

The Indians honored him with Razor Shines Appreciation Night
before the final home game of his final season on September 4. He
shed a tear during the pregame ceremony in which he was presented
with a new Chevy Lumina, courtesy of Payton-Wells Chevrolet, then
went out and had two big hits in a 13 – 4 victory over Louisville.

His leadoff double off the right field wall in the seventh inning
ignited a three-run rally that gave the Indians a 4 – 3 lead. He came
back with a one-out single in the eighth and scored the first run of a
nine-run rally.

He was lifted for a defensive replacement with two outs in the ninth
inning and left to a standing ovation from the crowd of 8,121.

The Indians still had two more games to play in Louisville to complete the season. We lost both of them to finish last in our division, but
Razor went out swinging. He contributed a two-run double in the first
of those games and two doubles in the last one.

He played 16 seasons, from Single-A to the Majors, from Mexico
City to Montreal. He won five championship rings with the Indianapolis Indians. After his playing career, he worked his way up through the
minor-league ranks as a coach and manager. He's managed nine different teams over 11 seasons in the minors, compiling more than 500
wins. He's also been a coach in the major-leagues for the White Sox
and Mets. Most recently, he worked as a coach in Taiwan.

Razor Shines has one of the most distinctive names in baseball,
and it happened to be one of the most appropriate as well. He always
played with an edge, and his energy and optimism lit up his teammates
and fans. 🟦

Michael Jordan put fans in seats despite never playing a game in our ballpark.

MICHAEL JORDAN

Michael Jordan, whom many people consider the greatest basketball player of all time, made a lot of money for other NBA teams during his playing career when he visited their arenas. He unknowingly made money for the Indianapolis Indians as well, without ever stepping foot in our stadium. Jordan left the NBA in 1993 to pursue a career in baseball. Citing burnout from leading the Chicago Bulls to three consecutive championships and fatigued by both his white-hot fame and his father's murder earlier that year, he sought a break from basketball and a new challenge. He took on the challenge of playing professional baseball, although he hadn't even played the sport in high school. He considered it a tribute to his father, who had envisioned him becoming a great baseball player when he was young

The White Sox signed Jordan to a contract and sent him to their Double-A team in Birmingham, Alabama. If he earned a promotion to their Triple-A affiliate in Nashville, Tennessee, he would play against the Indians in Indianapolis.

In anticipation of that possibility, people lit up our phone lines as the 1994 season approached, wanting to purchase tickets for our games against Nashville. I knew nobody, no matter how great an athlete he had been in another sport, could earn a spot in Triple A without a strong baseball background, but some of the callers were absolutely convinced Jordan could do it.

I instructed the people in our ticket department to tell every caller it was highly unlikely Jordan would ever play a game in Indianapolis. It was amazing the way some people argued with our reps, saying "Oh, no, he'll be here!" If people were persistent, we sold them the tickets they wanted, but at least they were warned of the unlikely odds of getting to see Jordan play.

As it turned out, Jordan never played baseball in Indianapolis or any other Triple-A city. He batted just .202 for Birmingham, then returned to the NBA on March 19, 1995—in Indianapolis against the Pacers, by the way. ◉

1994

T here's a story about the 1994 Indianapolis Indians team that won the American Association playoffs that captures the unique character of that group. ● The threat of a strike hung over Major League Baseball from the beginning of the '94 season, and eventually came to fruition when the season ended abruptly and prematurely on August 11.

Casey Candaele, a member of the Indians' championship team of 1986, had played in seven major-league seasons before 1994. The Reds had signed him as a free agent the previous November after his contract with Houston ran out, so he obviously was well-compensated at the time—probably about $300,000 for that season.

With the likelihood of a strike growing, Candaele asked our manager Marc Bombard at midseason to tell Reds management

Casey Candaele batted .282 in 131 games with the Indianapolis Indians in 1994.

of his strong desire to stay in Indianapolis. He would not have played much for them, so it was far better for him to stay with us, play nearly every game, and collect his paycheck.

Bombard reported back to Casey that the Reds had agreed to his request. But later, shortly before the strike deadline and with a walkout looking inevitable, Bombard called Casey into his office at Bush Stadium and told him the Reds were calling him up.

"I'm sorry, he said solemnly, "I did all I could do to convince them to keep you here, but they insisted on calling you up. These things happen sometimes; there was nothing I could do."

Casey went berserk, dancing around the clubhouse as if his shoes were on fire and screaming loudly and profanely. In so many words—in many words, actually—he complained that the Reds had lied to him.

It was a joke, however. Casey had been pranked. The other players loved it because he was usually the practical joker, the one who loved to tease his teammates. He was good at it and kept everyone loose, but this time he was on the butt end. He finally settled down after Bombard confessed.

That incident said a lot about the team's camaraderie and spirit, because teams lacking those qualities aren't likely to pull clever pranks on one another. It was full of players with major-league experience because the Reds had endured an injury-plagued season in 1993 and stocked their roster with free agents in the offseason. Bombard, who had been a pitcher and coach in the Reds organization as well as a minor-league manager, was the perfect man to lead them. He made solid in-game decisions and knew how to relate to the players.

That team's motto was "Refuse to Lose." It was a corny but sincere reflection of its rah-rah attitude, which flowed from Candaele more than anyone. He was a 5-foot-9, 160-pound second baseman, but made up for his lack of size with energy, spirit, and talent. He had proved that to us in 1986, when he batted .302 and was voted MVP for our championship team after beginning the season as a utility infielder.

Joe Sparks, the manager of that team, recalls Candaele showing up at the airport wearing a hodge-podge wardrobe of clothing he probably had picked up at a thrift store—such as red pants, a blue shirt, a green hat, and a silly tie—just for laughs. He also remembers Candaele tying popcorn boxes to his feet in Louisville and walking around the clubhouse in imitation of Razor Shines's distinctive strut.

Howard Kellman, our radio voice, tells of a doubleheader in Buffalo against the Bisons. Candaele walked on the team bus as it was about to leave for the ballpark and shouted, "Buffalo Bisons?! That's redundant! Let's beat them twice!"

Casey had baseball in his blood from his mother's side. He was one of five sons of Helen Callaghan Candaele, who played in the All-American Girls Professional Baseball League that sprang up during World War II while most of the male professionals were in the military. Casey's brother Kelly produced a documentary on the league, which was the inspiration for the 1992 movie, *A League of Their Own*.

The '94 season was as competitive as Triple-A baseball could be because other teams, like us, didn't have nearly as many call-ups as usual. Major-league teams wanted their prospects to be on the field, not on strike, and therefore were more reluctant to promote them. Blessed with experienced talent, we finished the regular season with an 86 – 57 record, swept Louisville in the first round of the playoffs, and won the championship series against Nashville, 3 – 1.

Bombard was named Manager of the Year, repeating the honor he had won two years earlier when he led Buffalo to an 87 – 57 record. He would also lead Indianapolis to a regular-season title in 1995, although that team lost in the first round of the playoffs.

The '94 championship was clinched with a 7 – 5 victory in front of 7,202 fans at Bush Stadium.

"Indianapolis has seen a lot of champions, but they'll never forget this one," Bombard said. "It's the best team I've ever been fortunate enough to manage—great makeup, a lot of character, unselfish, a lot of leaders."

Because of all the free agent signings in the offseason, our '94 team could have qualified as a solid major-league expansion club. It stayed intact, too, because the Reds had few injury issues before the strike, which further reduced the number of call-ups.

Candaele, who hit a first-inning home run in the title-clinching game, had played parts of seven major-league seasons.

Left fielder Kevin Maas, who hit a two-run homer in the second inning and was voted the playoff MVP, had played the previous four seasons with the Yankees.

Shortstop Kurt Stillwell contributed a double and two singles in the final game after hitting a three-run homer the previous night in Game Three, and batted .500 in the postseason. He had eight seasons of major-league experience and was a member of the American League All-Star team while with Kansas City in 1988.

Leadoff hitter William Pennyfeather, a right fielder, had a sacrifice fly and home run in the final game. He had played sparingly the previous two seasons with Pittsburgh before being released in May upon playing in four games with the Pirates.

Other major contributors with major-league backgrounds that season included outfielder Doug Jennings (Cubs), catcher Barry Lyons (Mets), and pitchers Rick Reed (Rangers) and Rich DeLucia (Mariners). Reed went seven innings and got the victory in the final game, and DeLucia pitched the final 1 1/3 innings for the save.

Bombard did a great job, too. My only complaint with him was that he used snuff. Baseball players and managers had been putting a pinch between their cheek and gums or chewing tobacco for decades, but the dangers had become well-known by the 1990s. Former major-league catcher and television personality Joe Garagiola visited teams throughout the country in the 1980s and '90s to promote his cause of tobacco abstinence. He had been a chewer in his playing days. He often took along an 11-season veteran, Bill Tuttle, who had undergone surgery to remove part of his jaw because of his addiction, which provided graphic evidence of the consequences.

Bombard was a coach with Cincinnati when Garagiola visited the Reds clubhouse in spring training. It didn't seem to have much impact, however. Later, I suggested that he give up the habit.

"This is America, isn't it?" he said. "I can use tobacco if I want to."

I said yes, he could, but suggested it might be a good idea to take the advice of his elders on this topic. I challenged him to break the habit over the winter months, when there was less stress in his world.

Or so I thought.

"I need it more when I'm home in the winter than during the season," he said.

Our championship offered Reds executives a brief but welcome respite from the frustrations of the strike. Our championship was clinched on the day the World Series was officially cancelled, a sad day for everyone in baseball. Reds owner Marge Schott attended our game and said afterward, "I haven't had a lot of good news today; this is the best I've had."

Schott, who owned the Reds from 1984 – 99, didn't come to our games often, but when she did it was a spectacle. As one of baseball's most unique and publicized figures, she attracted attention wherever she went. She always brought her St. Bernard, Schottzie II, with her, and we kept it in a doghouse out in left field foul territory.

Marge didn't want to be bothered during our games, but toward the end, she would tell the ushers to have her dog retrieved and to allow children to come down and get autographs. She even had a stamp of a dog's paw to give "autographs" from her dog.

A longtime smoker, she had her own issues with tobacco. She died in 2004 at the age of 75. Although a controversial figure, she got a lot of pleasure out of baseball—and the 1994 Indianapolis Indians were able to provide some of it. ●

HEADING DOWNTOWN

By the 1990s, it had become obvious the Indianapolis Indians needed a new ballpark. Our home of more than 60 years had been good to us, but was falling apart. We always referred to it as "beautiful Bush Stadium," but it was only beautiful in select areas. The grass on the field was green, ivy covered the outfield walls and the old-fashioned, hand-operated scoreboard in left field was a distinctive feature, similar to the ones in Wrigley Field in Chicago and Fenway Park in Boston.

The rest of the stadium was crumbling, however. The locker rooms in particular were substandard. Our players were always accepting of them, but they were small and poorly maintained. The same could be said for our public restrooms, especially for women.

Our offices weren't much better. Space was limited and we didn't have air conditioning for many years. When the sun was setting and glared directly through the windows on the west side of the stadium, it became horribly hot in the late afternoon. We eventually were able to purchase a few second-hand window units, which helped some, but that wasn't nearly as comfortable as central air conditioning.

I tried to get William Hudnut, who served as Indianapolis's mayor from 1976 – 1992, interested in building a new stadium for the city.

He was a friend and had shown interest in the team—especially when we won championships. He always made it a point to participate in the postgame locker room celebrations, pouring champagne on the players' heads and letting them do the same to him.

I could never convince him of the benefit a new stadium would have on Indianapolis, however. And if he wasn't interested, the Capital Improvement Board wasn't going to support the idea, either. It seemed we were stuck in a park that was crumbling around us.

Good things began to happen, though, when Stephen Goldsmith was elected to succeed Hudnut in November 1991. Just a month after Goldsmith was elected, I encountered him at a Kiwanis Club Christmas program. I pulled him aside and told him I wanted to talk to him about a new ballpark. He gave me an appointment in his office, we met, and right away he shared my vision of what a new facility could do for Downtown Indianapolis.

At his request we made the case for a new ballpark to various community groups by giving tours of Bush Stadium. One of our staff members, Dan Madden, led the way. Most people left midway through the tour after seeing all the decaying concrete and other areas of the rickety structure that seemed on the verge of falling down. They didn't need to see the complete tour to be convinced of the need for a new facility.

Obtaining a downtown location on which to build was no easy task, though. Governor Evan Bayh made that happen for us. He controlled the use of the White River State Park and enlisted the support of the White River State Park Commission. The land was made available at no charge to the Indians and the Capital Improvement Board (CIB). Eventually, it was established that the stadium would be leased to the CIB and subleased to the Indians.

Some people were opposed to a new ballpark because of their emotional attachment to Bush Stadium. Other disputed the downtown location in White River State Park. The *Indianapolis Star* published a letter from a woman who didn't think it appropriate for a ballpark to be built in a state park. The sentence from the letter I'll always remember is, "What is the highest and best use for that land?"

Highest and best use? The land designated for the Indians was being used as a gravel parking lot at the time. I knew we would be a much greater asset than that. I had traveled around the country and had seen firsthand what a new ballpark could be and what it could do for a city. I also knew our attendance would make a quantum leap forward and the game experience for our fans would improve dramatically.

As part of the transition, we worked out a new arrangement for maintenance with the CIB. The Parks Department had been responsible for maintenance at Bush Stadium, but that didn't work out well. Their penny-pinching philosophy, which was specifically stated to me, was to wait until something broke before fixing it. We wanted to be in control of the upkeep of the new stadium in order to engage in preventative maintenance. In exchange for becoming responsible for ballpark maintenance, we were allowed to keep all revenue from tickets, concessions, signage, and advertising.

That was important to us because, for a minor-league team, the ballpark is the most important asset for drawing fans—even more than

Indianapolis mayor Steve Goldsmith, Indians president and general manager Max Schumacher, Capitol Improvement board president Pat Early, and Indians board chairman Hank Warren broke ground for Victory Field on December 16, 1994.

winning. The major-league affiliate controls the roster, which changes dramatically from year to year. You are bound to have some losing seasons as a result, and it's mostly out of your control. But the park remains the same. It has to be kept clean, safe, and comfortable for the fans.

The city later imposed a 5% tax on our tickets, which felt like a low blow, but we couldn't do anything about that.

We had some hiccups during the construction phase of the stadium. Mayor Goldsmith moved the goal posts on us a few times, but that was understandable; he had to be responsible to the taxpayers of Indianapolis. We'd go down a certain road and think we were close to a deal and then he'd make a change.

It originally was to be a $20 million ballpark, but Mayor Goldsmith changed his mind and said we needed to keep the budget within $18 million. The city was to pay for half and the Indians the other half. Most of what we had to eliminate isn't noticeable to fans, though. We would have had improved access in some areas, more room for storage and a better heating and cooling system if not for the cuts.

Our discussions of the construction details—which included "value engineering" topics that were a great frustration—were conducted primarily with Capital Improvement Board President Pat Early, who was an enthusiastic booster of the project. Indians board member Michael Browning contributed financial and construction expertise at no charge.

I originally wanted the stadium capacity to be 20,000. We settled for 13,300 permanent seats, with lawn seating available for more than 2,000 fans. Later, we removed about 1,000 bleacher seats to make room for a picnic area.

That's the right capacity for us. We still have the second-largest park in Triple-A baseball, behind only Buffalo. Its stadium, Coca Cola Field, seats just over 18,000 fans. I had wanted to surpass Buffalo, but I admit to letting my competitive instincts get the best of me and overestimating our needs.

The new ballpark opened on July 11, 1996. We had to go without offices the first season because Mayor Goldsmith was getting anxious and wanted to get it opened that year. The architects came to us in March and said they could get it done if they didn't finish everything. We said OK.

They came back to us with a list and said, "Can you do without suites?"

No, we've sold all the suites.

"Well, what about concession stands?"

No, we need to sell popcorn and beer.

"What about your offices?"

We agreed to put that off. Some of us stayed at Bush Stadium and drove back and forth between the old and new parks. We also had a trailer set up in the parking lot of the new stadium where some people could work. I set up a makeshift office in the Indians Suite at the new park. I'd work at Bush Stadium in the morning, eat a fast food sandwich on the way downtown, and set up a typewriter on the bar to continue working. I had a phone, and that was all I really needed.

The move to Victory Field has been successful on all counts. It has been voted the best minor-league ballpark in the country and remains one of the best after more than 20 years of operation. It also dramatically improved the Indians' financial status. The franchise has been profitable every season since 1975, but a new threshold was reached after the move.

More than anything, it has proven to be a great addition to Downtown Indianapolis, bringing people there who spend money at restaurants and other businesses near the park.

I had emphasized that point to Mayor Goldsmith during our negotiations. Two or three years after we opened the park, he told me, "You know what you told me Victory Field would do for Indianapolis? It has done that." I am indebted to him for sharing my vision and pushing it forward.

Since making the move downtown, numerous fans have approached me and said, "When you were talking about the new ballpark, I wasn't for you. I loved Bush Stadium, and I didn't think I could ever love a ballpark as well as Bush Stadium—until I saw Victory Field."

By the way, that name means something to us. One of the few things we insisted upon in our lease with the city was owning the naming rights to the stadium. We didn't want it to be sold to a corporation and have some schlock name attached to it. We wanted Victory Field, which had been used for the old stadium.

Our former home had been named Perry Stadium when it was built in 1931, because it was built by a man named Norm Perry as a memorial to his brother, James, who had been killed in a light plane crash near Ft. Benjamin Harrison. The construction cost was $350,000.

Mr. Perry later agreed to sell the franchise to Frank McKinney Sr. and Ownie Bush. The papers were signed on December 6, 1941, a Saturday. Pearl Harbor was bombed the next day. That inspired fans to vote to rename the stadium Victory-something—park, stadium, whatever. Victory Field ultimately won out.

The name was changed to Bush Stadium in November of 1967 after the city purchased the park for about $300,000—$50,000 below its construction cost in the Depression era—from the estate of Mr. Perry. The city wanted to honor Ownie Bush for all he had done for baseball in the city, so the stadium was named after him at the time of the sale. The purchase was made with a bond that was to be paid off after 10 years, but the Bush Stadium Commission was unable to make the lease payments. Indianapolis' new mayor Richard G. Lugar appointed a special task force, headed by Harry T. Ice, which came up with a workable plan.

Even after the sale and name change, a lot of people continued to call the stadium Victory Field, either out of habit or preference. That name was originally adopted to declare the intent to emerge victorious during World War II, but it relates to victory in baseball, too. We didn't feel the need to have a contest to come up with a name when we built the new downtown stadium, we just went back to that great historical name.

It's still the perfect name today, and the Indians are committed to keeping it.

SO LONG, CINCINNATI (AGAIN)

I've always been outspoken, maybe at times too outspoken, when I thought the Indians were being treated unfairly. I considered myself a representative for the fans in Indianapolis, and it was my responsibility to stand up for them when necessary. ● It became necessary again in 1999, and it led to a third ugly breakup with the Reds.

Our relationship had become strained the previous season when I believed they failed to provide us with adequate replacements after they called up some of our key players. We ultimately missed the play-offs—by a half-game—for the first time since 1993 despite holding an eight-game lead in our division in mid-July.

I aired an objection in the *Indianapolis Star* at the end of the season, stating that if the Reds handled the things the same way the following season, it would be an indication they didn't want to work with us any longer.

The 1999 season, the final one on our contract with the Reds, deteriorated quickly. In June, the Star's beat writer covering the Indians Phillip B. Wilson approached me at a game with a copy of an article that had appeared in *The Cincinnati Post* a week earlier. The last paragraph read, "[Reds] officials would like to move out of Indianapolis and into Louisville." The article also reported "high-ranking Reds sources made off-the-record inferences about a possible change a month ago."

I was stunned by the news, and angry that nobody from the Reds had called me, especially after the article had appeared in the newspaper.

Doc Rogers, the Reds' assistant general manager, denied the report. "We love Indy, and we think Indy loves us," he said. "In a perfect marriage, you don't look for another partner." I called Bowden myself, and he made a similar statement to me.

It was hardly a perfect marriage, though, and it only got worse. At one point in the season, our general manager Cal Burleson got into a heated argument with Bowden behind the batting cage before one of our games. It was a credit to Cal's integrity that he offered to resign if that would save our relationship with the Reds, but I had no interest in that. Cal was passionate about the Indians and doing a great job.

Besides, I agreed with him. I angered Bowden myself later that season when I gave an interview to a local television reporter, Russ McQuaid, and stated my frustration with the Reds' personnel decisions that affected us.

It was bad enough the Reds were secretly negotiating with Louisville without our knowledge, but it also was a violation of a Major League Baseball rule enacted in 1991 that prohibited teams from discussing affiliation changes before September 6. Teams operating on an expiring contract are to notify the Major League Baseball office and the minor-league offices if they want to file for a reaffiliation. Brewers general manager Dean Taylor and International League president Randy Mobley agreed that the Reds violated the rule.

Lo and behold, when the lists of teams wanting a reaffiliation came out in September, Cincinnati and Louisville both were on it. They immediately announced their agreement, leaving us with no choice but to replace Louisville as Milwaukee's Triple-A affiliate.

We filed a grievance with the primary intent of saving our relationship with the Reds, which was our fan's preference, but received no response. That type of conflict just wasn't high on the list of priorities for MLB.

It didn't excite our fans, as the Brewers had no significant following in Indianapolis. But, like the previous times we parted company with the Reds, it turned out to be a good move for us—at least in the short term. ●

Max introduced Cecil Cooper, who was Indianapolis's manager in 2003 and '04, at a preseason banquet.

2000

We basically had an arranged marriage with Milwaukee. Once the Reds hooked up with Louisville, the Brewers were without a Triple-A affiliate and we were without a major-league affiliate. Neither of us had a choice but to get together. So, despite the disappointment of many fans over the loss of our relationship with Cincinnati, we dug in and tried to make the best of it. And it worked out for the best, as we won the Triple-A World Series in the 2000 season.

I would be lying if I didn't admit to savoring that victory a little more than most, given the nature of our split with the Reds the previous season. We were like a spurned lover who winds up with a better partner—at least for a while.

Milwaukee's general manager Dean Taylor was a great guy and an excellent general manager, and we got along well with farm director Greg Riddoch as well. Steve Smith was hired to be our manager. We didn't have a choice in the matter. Unlike early in my career, when I could have a say in hiring a new manager, by this time major-league teams would say, "We've got a guy we think will do a good job for you. Do you know him?" If we said no, they said, "Well, I think you'll like him."

We did like him, it turned out. Smith, 46 years old at the time, had a wealth of experience as a major-league coach, minor-league coach, and manager; he was the Seattle Mariners' third-base coach before coming to us. He was a self-proclaimed "surfer dude" from southern California, but also a college-educated family man and fitness buff who worked as an extra in movies and television during the offseason. Consistent with his outgoing nature and active lifestyle, he took a hands-on role with the players in practice and coached third base in games.

We started the season quickly and finished with an 81 – 63 regular-season record. Milwaukee's front office did a great job for us, stocking our roster with veterans who would much rather have been playing in the Majors but still led us to the championship.

Outfielder Lyle Mouton was the best example. He was 31 years old and had played in 307 major-league games before joining us on July 1. I told Dean Taylor later in the season that we might be able to win a championship if he would leave Mouton with us the rest of the way, and he did. Mouton batted .305 with 12 home runs in 51 games with us, and got two things he wouldn't have achieved with the Brewers: extensive playing time and the only championship ring of his career.

Catcher Creighton Gubanich was 28 years old and had played in 18 games with the Boston Red Sox the previous season. He batted .284 with 16 home runs with us. First baseman Kurt Bierek, also 28, led us with 19 home runs and 72 RBI. Relief pitcher Bob Scanlan was 31 years old and had pitched more than 500 major-league innings. He was our team MVP and set an Indians record with 35 saves.

The Indians won the International League's West Division—finishing 10 games ahead of the Reds' affiliate in Louisville, by the way. We defeated South Division winner Durham in the first round of the playoffs, then Scranton/Wilkes Barre from the North Division to capture the International League championship.

We then took on Memphis in Las Vegas for the Triple-A championship and won that series, 3 – 1. Shortstop Santiago Perez was voted the series MVP after collecting six hits and two home runs in 13 at-bats. Scanlan, appropriately, pitched a perfect inning to clinch the victory in the final game.

The Memphis roster, by the way, included a 20-year-old prospect named Albert Pujols. The future three-time National League MVP rose quickly through the St. Louis ranks in his only minor-league season, breezing through the Single-A and Double-A levels to play the final three games of the regular season for Memphis and join them for the playoffs.

Santiago Perez was a key member of the championship team in 2000.

The season was a financial success as well. We drew more than 650,000 fans, helping people to quickly forget the Reds. But as is so often the case in minor league baseball, things changed quickly. Steve Smith headed straight from Las Vegas for his home in San Diego and didn't return as our manager. He had agreed with the Brewers before the season began that he would take the assignment for just one season before becoming a roving infield instructor.

Our relationship with Milwaukee's front office gradually deteriorated. They made several front office changes in 2002, which was painful for me because of my close relationship with the people I had worked with. I had a lot of respect for Bob Melvin, the new general manager, but didn't connect as well with the new farm director, Reid Nichols, who replaced Greg Riddoch.

I recall one afternoon game when it began raining. I walked down to the box seat area where Nichols was supposed to be sitting to ask if he wanted to come sit in one of the suites, but couldn't find him. I then called the hotel where he was staying, and he picked up the phone. He thought it was a night game.

Our rapport with the Brewers' front office was declining and our talent pool was growing shallow. After that championship in 2000, the

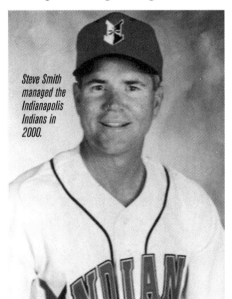

Steve Smith managed the Indianapolis Indians in 2000.

Indians posted four consecutive losing seasons, winning between 64 and 66 games each year.

I also was unhappy with the Brewers' bookkeeping in 2004. They had begun to keep some of their injured minor-league players on our active list to shrink their disabled list payroll. That satisfied their accountants, but "active" players that couldn't play weren't helping us win, and I didn't appreciate the subterfuge.

Once again, it was time to move on.

I made one call in search of a new Major League affiliate: to Pittsburgh Pirates general manager David Littlefield. The Pirates' organization was filled with good prospects at the Double-A level in Altoona, Pennsylvania, like Ryan Doumit, Zach Duke, Nate McLouth, and Ian Snell, would be with us the following season.

The Pirates, meanwhile, were eager to work with us after a seven-year run with Nashville in the Pacific Coast League. At the very least we were more geographically desirable. And, our parks were similar in their dimensions, putting premiums on good defensive leftfielders and centerfielders.

It has proved to be a good partnership, as we're still affiliates today. Future Pirates stars like Andrew McCutchen, Gregory Polanco, Starling Marte, and Josh Bell have played in Indianapolis on their way to the big leagues. ●

THE FRONT OFFICE

I experienced the front office from both ends of the spectrum—as a new employee who did what I was told, and as the boss who told others what to do. In either case, my experience was educational and nearly always enjoyable. In later years, I took great pride in helping young employees build a career, whether it was with the Indians or somewhere else. I always told them not to stay too long if working for a baseball team wasn't their first love. Sometimes people get comfortable in a job and settle into it even though they would rather be doing something else. I didn't want anyone to have regrets, both for personal and professional reasons. While I wanted everyone to have a fulfilling career, I also knew frustrated or bored employees didn't perform as well.

I knew from the moment I began working for the Indians in 1957 that I wanted to stay as long as I could. I didn't realize I would have the opportunity to become the general manager as early as I did, but I never had a foot out the door.

The atmosphere when I began working was more relaxed than professional. A couple of months after joining the Indians, I was asked by

Bob Weimer, our business manager, to come to his office. I grabbed a pad of paper and a pen, expecting to be given instructions of some sort.

"Are you a gin rummy player?" he asked.

"No," I said. "I like to play cards, but I don't know how to play gin rummy."

"Well, you're going to learn," he said.

Ray Johnston, the general manager, had left the office early that afternoon so Bob wanted to knock off work and play. But Ray forgot something and doubled back to the office and caught us in the act. It turned out that he had warned Bob about playing cards on company time before, so he called him to a back room and scolded him again.

It didn't make a difference. Bob played gin at every opportunity, and I had little choice but to join him. It didn't take much persuasion, I'll admit.

Various people passed through the games, such as Norm Beplay, our public address announcer, Coach Johnny Hutchings, and occasionally a player or two. We played for loose change, basically, a quarter or 50 cents per game. We put the winnings into a kitty and then all went to a show at Starlight Musicals in the spring with the proceeds.

Hutchings was fun to have in the games because he wasn't very good. He was so good-natured, though, he laughed along with us when we teased him. He once said, "You might have beat me today, but if you kept standings you'd find out who the better player is."

So we kept standings. He was the worst player.

I happened to be the best player that particular year and was awarded a trophy—with my name misspelled. I kept it in my office until I retired, and refused to let it go until I moved out of my longtime home and into a senior community.

I gained a reputation as a good gin player, so someone issued a challenge to White Sox announcer Bob Elson when our major-league affiliate was in town for a midseason exhibition game in 1959. We squared off in the Perry Room at the stadium afterward while the players were showering and dressing.

I won. I hadn't realized we were playing for money, but Bob did some figuring and told me he owed me a little more than seven dollars. He pulled a $100 bill out of his wallet and handed it to me and asked for change. It reminded me of the customers on my newspaper route as a kid who would give me a $20 bill and then tell me they would catch me next time when I didn't have enough change—and hope to get out of ever making the payment.

I probably surprised Bob when I handed the bill to Bob Weimer, who went into our vault containing petty cash and returned with the proper change.

That moment became public the following spring at our downtown preseason banquet sponsored by the Jaycees. Milo Hamilton, Elson's sidekick in the broadcasting booth, was brought in as the guest speaker and told everyone how Elson liked to pay off his gin debts with $100 bills, hoping to get out of it.

"But Schumacher, he opens the vault!" Milo said.

The gin games were conducted only through the winter months, in the late afternoon hours when the front office was less hectic. It was easy to knock off work early then, because few things had to be done at that moment, unlike the faster pace during the season. You could always put off a task for another day.

If you're wondering if the gin games continued after I became the general manager in 1961, the answer is an absolute no. The truth is, you always had work to do in the winter months. There always was another person to contact in hopes of selling a ticket or sponsorship or program advertisement.

I liked to play. But I didn't want anyone playing under my watch.

Plenty of issues more serious than gin games came up during my years in the front office.

We had a business manager named Terry Stewart. He had been working in the ticket office for the St. Louis Cardinals but was looking for a new opportunity, and I hired him to work for the Indians.

Terry was a good-looking bachelor who, to his credit, had high moral standards. He proved that to me in 1970 when pitcher Bo Belinsky joined the Indians in an attempt to revive his major-league career.

Bo had been an overnight, but brief, sensation as a rookie with the Los Angeles Angels in 1962 when he won his first four games and capped off the streak with a no-hitter. He was an unabashed playboy, though, who wound up having a rocky career. By the time he got to us in 1970, he was 33 years old and past his prime. He went 7 – 6 with a 4.45 earned run average for the Indians, and never returned to the Majors.

Bo was newly married to Jo Collins, a former Playboy bunny who had appeared in the magazine as a playmate. When the Indians were on road trips, she would come in and flirt with Terry, trying to entice him into getting together. Bo was famous for doing the same kind of thing, though, and didn't try hard to hide it. Terry never did go on a date with her, and didn't even give her encouragement. He said he had made a vow that he would never date a married woman.

He wasn't as dedicated to baseball, though. In 1978 we were dependent on Iowa beating Evansville late in the season to qualify for the playoffs. If nothing else, having playoff games would improve our financial status. After Iowa won, we all celebrated.

Everyone but Terry, that is. He shook the walls by slamming shut the door to our vault, because he was angry over having to work deeper into the fall.

Terry also didn't care much for young children. He was a bachelor, so he wasn't accustomed to being around them. One of his responsibilities was to keep order in the seating areas and not let kids run all over the place. That wasn't always easy.

Ken Griffey Sr. played for us in 1973 and '74. He and his wife, Alberta ("Bertie") had a son, Ken Jr. He was an energetic little kid, four or five years old. His mom would sit with the other wives behind home plate, but pretty soon Junior was off on his own, looking for fun. Terry warned Mrs. Griffey about letting him roam around the park, but it didn't do much good.

One night Ken Jr. was running on the concourse behind the stands along the left field foul line, which threatened to irritate the fans walking to the concession stands or restrooms and created the threat of an injury. Terry grabbed him, marched him down to Mrs. Griffey, and laid down the law to her. "I've talked to you about keeping an eye on your kid! Put him in a seat and keep him there!"

Ken Jr. of course went on to become a multimillion dollar player and a Hall of Famer, and here we had him by the scruff of the neck dragging him back to mommy.

I wish Terry had been as aggressive as a salesman. Back then, I tried to get all staff members to sell tickets, sponsorships, and advertising as well as perform their office duties. We had a small sales staff, but I wanted staff members taking advantage of their contacts in the community to sell anything that brought revenue to the team. We had such severe financial problems in those days and had to do that to survive.

I couldn't get Terry to sell, though. One year we had lost some of our staff members and I needed Terry to help me with some accounts that had historically been renewed each fall. It was as simple as making a call and writing up an order, usually, but he wouldn't do it. Then, when he came in on a Friday later that fall and announced he was going on vacation and would be back in three weeks, it was enough. I called him into my office and asked him to sit down.

"Terry, I'm going to have to let you go," I said.

"Why, because I won't sell?" he asked.

"Yes. We're shorthanded in the ticket department, and we're trying to stay in business. I need your help, and you're not willing to help."

After I fired Terry, he went to work for the Ross and Babcock ticket agency and later in the Indiana Pacers' ticket department. I was frustrated with him, but he was honest. A lot of money passed through his hands, but I never questioned whether he stole a penny from the Indians.

I can't say that about everyone.

At one point, we started coming up short of cash in our ticket office. Everyone working there thought it was a new employee, a young woman. A lot of days she would eat lunch with her boyfriend as they sat in his car in the parking lot. That aroused suspicion because she could easily pass along money from the office to him at that time.

I called a meeting and told everyone about the situation. I said I needed to find out who was guilty and that we were going to have polygraph examinations for everyone working in the ticket office.

I occasionally worked in there myself when we were really busy, helping to answer phones and greet the public, so I said I should have to take the examination, too. I told the young woman, "You and I will be the first to take the examination. The man's coming tomorrow with his equipment."

She didn't show up for work the following morning. In fact, she never even came back to get her paycheck. We didn't need the lie detector test after all—which was a good thing, because I was bluffing. Had she shown up the next day, I would have had to arrange for someone to come out and administer a test.

People like that were the exception rather than the rule, however. The vast majority of our front office employees have been intelligent, dedicated, and ethical. And while you might make an occasional hiring mistake, you also benefit from occasions when a good employee falls into your lap.

People in charge of hiring for professional sports teams get a lot of requests from professional acquaintances to hire their friends or relatives. Hank Peters, who was the president of minor league baseball—formally known as the National Association of Professional Baseball Leagues—from 1972 – 75, asked me once to bring his son to Indianapolis to work in our front office. I had already hired a couple of people, though, and couldn't fit him in. Sheldon "Chief" Bender of the Reds had already asked me to hire his son, Jim, as business manager, and I had agreed.

That turned out to be a mistake. But I caught a break.

Our winter meetings were in New Orleans that same year, and that's where I met Cal Burleson. Cal was walking the halls of the hotel, trying to land a job in minor league baseball. I had to tell him we didn't have an opening. Cal was tenacious, though. He's a great researcher by nature and did his homework on the Indians franchise. He might have pursued other teams, too, but he knew what we were about and that he wanted to work for us.

He always seemed to be standing in a doorway during those meet-ings, selling himself to me. I kept explaining that I didn't have any money left in the budget to pay him a salary, but he offered me a deal I couldn't refuse. He was willing to come on as a commission-only ticket salesman.

Cal had a bachelor's degree as well as a master's degree in sports administration from Ohio University. He had worked a year for the Jacksonville minor-league team before attending that meeting in New Orleans. He was frustrated in that job because he couldn't get out of

Cal Burleson, at left with manager Steve Smith in 2000, held the 2000 Triple-A World Series trophy.

the office to sell, and here I was, frustrated because I couldn't get Jim Bender out of the office to sell.

Cal moved to Indianapolis, where he didn't know anybody, and had the guts to go out and sell. He did very well at it, too, and gradually advanced to better positions with a salary and more authority. He became Vice-President of the Indians and now works for the team as a consultant. He stands as a testament of getting into professional sports when you lack connections.

○

The workdays during the season are often long, but they can be fun— even without gin rummy games.

Kurt Hunt was one of our employees who helped make them that way. He joined us in the fall of 1979 after graduating from Butler with a Marketing degree. He jokes now about the fact he was left all alone by his third day on the job because the other full-time employees were attending the winter baseball meetings. Here he was, brand new to the job, and he's locking up Bush Stadium at the end of the day. It wasn't long before he was walking around the field and clubhouse with complete freedom, amazed at the sudden change in his life.

Kurt had a great sense of humor. He later became known to our fans as the public address announcer who invented the unique introduction of Razor Shines, which stayed with Razor throughout the rest of his career with the Indians. But I remember him for his duck costume.

There was a stretch during one of our seasons in the early 1980s when we were rained out for several consecutive days. Our routine became to show up for work in the morning, watch the weather radar, go to lunch, then return to the office and call off that night's game.

Kurt, who by then was our business manager, finally decided to do something about everyone's dampened enthusiasm. He rented a duck suit for about $30, put it on and walked into the office. I was sitting at my desk when he walked up in the costume with an Indians jersey slipped over the top. I'm told I about fell out of my chair when I first saw him.

He wore it the rest of the day in the office, without the head of course, and then went down to the playing field to greet the players as they arrived for a game that would not be played. Kurt exemplified the spirit you want from your front office employees. He worked hard, he had fun with the job, and he was innovative.

○

Each of my four children worked for the Indians at various times, but it never created a problem because I showed them no favoritism, and they worked hard. They all probably were underpaid for their work, but it was important that nobody believed they were getting preferential treatment.

For proof, I could point to the Sunday afternoon game in the 1970s

Bruce (left), Max (right), and Mark (bottom) Schumacher at Victory Field.

when I took my three oldest kids—Bruce, Brian, and Karen—with me to the park. I liked for them to go to those games because the atmosphere was more relaxed, and they were good about staying out of trouble.

This time, however, we walked into the park only to see trash spread all around the lower seating areas. The cleanup crew had blown all the paper cups, plates, and wrappers down from the upper areas following the previous night's game, but hadn't bothered to pick it up and haul it out. It was a huge mess, and we had a game coming up at 1:30 p.m.

"I'm sorry kids, but this is the problem you have when your last name is Schumacher," I said. "We have a crowd coming in two hours, and we have to clean this up."

We got unexpected help from Russ Nixon, who had been a catcher on Indianapolis' championship team in 1956. He was working in the Reds' front office at the time and arrived early to scout that day's game. Upon seeing our predicament, he rolled up his sleeves and began helping us. It was no small task, but he stayed with it until we finished.

With that kind of humble nature and work ethic, it's no wonder he had such a long career in baseball.

Bruce, my oldest child, is now the Indians' Chief Executive Officer and Chairman of the Board. He started out as the ticket manager in 1983, just as I had done in 1957, upon graduating from Indiana University in 1982. I held him back from promotions to avoid the impression of nepotism. I also wanted him to learn the business thoroughly.

Among his varied duties over the years before he was a full-time employee, was shooting videos of our pitchers for the Reds while we were their affiliate. He would only shoot our pitchers, so the Reds could have a better idea of how their prospects were performing and what mechanics might need improvement. He set up behind the backstop screen and was paid about $25 per game.

Brian did the same, but he didn't have as much interest in working full time in baseball. He still records balls and strikes for the scoreboard during games and has compiled statistics for historical references.

My daughter Karen used to run scores out to the people working behind our outfield scoreboard when the telephone service wasn't working, which was often. She also helped with mailings and worked inside the scoreboard, which was much like the old hand-operated scoreboards in Wrigley Field in Chicago and Fenway Park in Boston.

That might sound like a fun job, but it wasn't nearly as glamorous as it might seem. Rats often took up residence in the scoreboard, and it was really hot in there during the warmer summer months. We usually had two kids working in there, one on the upper level and one on the lower, and they would post the numbers to update the score of our game and provide scores of other games around the country.

She was an outstanding softball player in high school and became a police officer in Florida after graduating from Ball State.

Our youngest son, Mark, is now in charge of merchandise sales. He started out as an intern, as did most of our full-time employees. In fact, Randy Lewandowski, our current team president and general manager, was part of the same group of paid interns who began working full time when we moved to our downtown park. The others were Mark Walpole, Tim Harms, Chris Herndon, and Brad Morris.

My son Mark began attending games with Judy as an infant. As a growing boy, he was fascinated with the work performed by the grounds crew, particularly covering and uncovering the infield with the tarp. He even played with a "tarp" at home, taking a blanket and moving it to various places in the family room to keep them dry.

In my early years as the general manager, I usually listened to the road games on the radio. One night when Mark was about eight years old, I was enjoying what appeared to be a developing victory in Omaha when Royals outfielder Bombo Rivera hit a walk-off home run. I exploded in anger and kicked one of Mark's toys across the room.

From that time forward, whenever we listened on the radio and the Indians appeared to be in danger of losing a close game, Mark placed a Nerf football next to my right foot in case Dad lost his temper again.

When Mark was about 10 years old, it became time for him to begin his own work experiences at the ballpark. One day when we arrived at the ballpark, the grounds crew was removing the tarp from the field as we walked into the stadium. I thought it was a good time for him to help with the work that had always fascinated him, so I sent him out to help. He took a position on the right end of the cylinder on which the tarp was rolled and began pushing as hard as he could.

Upon reaching its stationary position, the cylinder stalled and Mark was thrust upward and over, landing head-first between the tarp and the box seat wall. He wasn't injured, suffering just a small cut on his face, but it scared me to death.

Eddie Dick, our tobacco-chewing groundskeeper, didn't share my concern, though. He just laughed and said, "It'll make a man out of him."

Easy for him to say.

○

One of the greatest pleasures I took from being a general manager was the opportunity to help young people advance their careers and find happy professional lives.

One example would be Ron McClain.

He was a student at Indiana University, studying to become an athletic trainer. He had worked with some of the teams there as well as at a local high school, and was hoping to land a full-time job upon graduation.

He was driving a delivery truck for $8.89 an hour in the summer of 1973, a really nice wage for a summer job at that time. He had ambition, though, so one afternoon he stopped by my office and asked if he could assist our trainer, Jimmy Bell, to gain experience. I told him I couldn't pay him, but as our conversation evolved we agreed he could assist on the grounds crew and help and observe Jimmy as time permitted.

He drove the truck on weekdays, and our games were played in the evenings or on weekend days, so he was able to do both jobs. Our manager, Vern Rapp, didn't want a young kid like that in the clubhouse during games at first, so Ron was just a gofer who performed jobs such as cleaning the whirlpool. He had strict orders not to work on any of the players.

But it so happened that Jimmy went home to Tulsa during our All-Star break that summer. While there, he learned University of Tulsa's head trainer had just died, and he was offered the job. He came back to me and said, "I know it's midseason, and I hate to do this to you, but I'd really like to take that job."

I thought about it for a few days and then talked to the Reds' front office. They agreed to let Bell out of his contract and, just like that, Ron became our trainer on an interim basis. I checked with Vern Rapp to see if he had confidence Ron could do the job for the final six weeks of the season. He talked with Ken Griffey Sr. and Rawly Eastwick, and they basically said, "He can't hurt anybody; he'll probably be all right."

Ron was able to complete his degree requirements at IU during our offseasons while beginning his career with us as a full-time trainer. Naturally, he had a lot to learn when he began. The first time he ever flew on an airplane was for our road trip to Denver, and he turned that one into quite an adventure. Trainers are in charge of luggage on road trips, and he had all of our equipment bags tagged with Chicago as the final destination. After all, that was the destination of that particular flight. After arriving in Chicago, he asked Vern how the airline personnel were going to know to send everything on to Denver, and that's when he learned how transporting luggage works. Ron had to go with three members of the airline's baggage crew to haul all the bags to a ticket counter and retag them for Denver.

He did a great job for us, though. In 1979 I got a call from John McHale, the Montreal Expos' general manager. We weren't affiliated with them yet, but we were friends. He had lost his trainer and he wanted to know if I could recommend anyone for the job. I didn't want to lose Ron, but it would have been selfish of me not to pass along his name.

Ron got the job. He was in the right place at the right time, but had earned the opportunity with his initiative and hard work, and I was happy to help make it happen. Montreal got a good trainer and Ron got to fulfill his dream. He worked for the Expos for 25 years before retiring and now has a great pension from Major League Baseball that will allow him and his family to be comfortable in retirement.

After the 1994 season, when the possibility of building a new downtown ballpark was looking more and more likely. I knew we were going to need a larger front office staff if it happened. I called in our interns to tell them that discussions were going well, and I was confident if they stayed on as paid interns for one more year, they each would have a full-time job in 1996.

From that group, a few of them are still with the team. My son, Mark, is the director of merchandising; Brad Morris is the senior director of business operations; and Randy Lewandowski is the president and general manager.

Experiences such as that more than make up for whatever problems you encounter in the front office. ●

PINCH HITS

I found the off-season league meetings I attended to be interesting and informative, but some were dramatic as well—such as the one where a man got punched and another that featured a screaming match that led to a law-suit. ● A. Ray Smith had a knack for keeping them in-teresting. He was confrontational and political by nature, and always seemed to be trying to manipulate someone to serve his own interests. He was a World War II veteran and graduate of Indiana University's business school who became wealthy as the owner of a construction compa-ny. He purchased Tulsa's Double-A franchise in 1961 and moved it into the Pacific Coast League in 1966.

He moved his franchise to New Orleans; Springfield, Illinois; then to Louisville for the 1982 season. He drummed up a lot of national publicity for himself by claiming to have drawn a million fans, and was voted the minor league Executive of the Year in 1982 and '83.

In those days, we shared revenue in the playoffs, with 45 percent of ticket sales going to the visiting team, 10 percent to the league, and the remaining 45 percent staying with the home team. For that reason, we all were salivating at the opportunity to play Louisville in the playoffs. But after we played the Redbirds in the 1984 postseason, we sent them a bigger check than they sent us. Smith had run a coupon in the Sunday newspaper that served as a free ticket to the game so we didn't benefit from that. But, of course, he got to keep 100 percent of all the concession and souvenir revenues generated by the fans who got in for free.

That was how he did business. That practice angered league general managers enough that we eventually changed the rules so that the home team kept all the revenues from playoff games.

My most vivid memory of him is from a league meeting in Springfield, when he was requesting league approval to move his team to Louisville. Ray Johnston, the former Indians general manager who owned the Iowa franchise, was pressing him hard, probing for information. A. Ray didn't like having to answer questions, as is typical of people who are promoters first and foremost.

Later, during a break in the meeting, Denver general manager Jim Burris and I were sitting next to one another at a table. A. Ray stuck his head between us and said, "I just want you guys to know, I slugged Ray Johnston in the men's room. I popped him a good one."

For emphasis, A. Ray slammed his right fist into his left palm.

"He's OK, though," he added. "I caught him before he hit the floor."

Most of A. Ray's attempts to manipulate people were less violent. One year, he brought to the league meeting a deal with Budweiser to sponsor telecasts of a few of our league games. That was to his credit; I don't believe anyone else could have arranged a television deal for the league. But A. Ray tried to use that as a bargaining chip to get favors from American Association president Joe Ryan.

A. Ray stood up and stated Joe had done a great job in helping negotiate the contract, and that instead of dividing the proceeds eight ways for each team to benefit, we should split it nine ways and give a share to Joe. That, of course, lessened the amount each team would receive. The truth was, Joe had nothing to do with the Budweiser deal, but A. Ray was trying to convince everyone Joe had significantly helped.

I'll never forget the presentation of Patty Cox Hampton, a distinguished silver-haired older lady who was owner and president of the Oklahoma City franchise. She and her husband, Bing, had saved the

89ers franchise by investing in it, and then built it into a successful enterprise. I never heard her say a bad word about anyone or use any form of profanity. But she stood up at the meeting and declared, "I've observed this, and Joe Ryan has done one *helluva job* in putting together this deal, and should receive a share of the rights fee."

A. Ray had fooled her into voting against her own best financial interests.

He didn't fool the rest of us, though. We voted to split the rights fee for the sponsorship deal eight ways instead of nine. It wasn't for a great deal of money, but every dollar counted, and one-eighth is more than one-ninth. Since 1998, the Indianapolis Indians have been a member of the International League under the outstanding and even-handed leadership of President Randy Mobley. Young league members today don't know how good they have it.

One of A. Ray's failed attempts to intimidate revealed a bright future for one notable baseball figure. Dave Drombrowski was the ad-

Max sat with American Association president Joe Ryan at a game in 1976.

ministrative assistant of the Chicago White Sox' minor-league organization in the late 1970s and attended our winter meeting. A. Ray thought he had fresh meat to manipulate and attempted his usual bullying tactics, but Dave stood his ground in a professional manner.

I knew then that he was someone who would go far in baseball administration. He became the Montreal general manager at age 31 and later became the general manager and president of the Florida Marlins and Detroit Tigers. He's been the President of Baseball Operations for the Boston Red Sox since 2015 and put together the team that won the World Series in 2018.

○

Another memorable winter meetings encounter occurred in December of 1981 in Hollywood, Florida. We had a morning meeting, with the game schedule as the primary topic. As some of the general managers waited for the start of the meeting, a few others arrived later with Joe Ryan. This cabal had met privately the previous night and made changes to the schedule for their own benefit. Several erasures were clearly visible on the draft of the schedule they brought with them.

Jim Burris, general manager of the Denver Bears, was sitting to my right. He began shouting at Wichita's GM Dick King who had been part of the privileged group, and accused him of tampering. The argument became heated as other disagreements arose and Burris—who I had always considered a fair-minded gentleman and an ally of mine in league matters—began shouting insults at King. He called him a "damn fat fag," "fatso," and "liar," all while pointing a green Sprite bottle at King. I was expecting King to come across the table at Burris, and preparing to break up a fight.

King later filed a $7 million lawsuit, alleging he had resigned his position with Wichita as a result of Burris' actions. He claimed severe financial losses, damage to his reputation, and severe emotional distress.

The issue was not settled until June 14, 1984, when a District Court judge in Denver ruled in Burris's favor and awarded no damages to King. Both sides had to pay their own legal fees.

○

The Indianapolis Indians are grateful for any amount of coverage we can get from the local media. The newspapers and broadcast outlets aren't as well-staffed as they once were, so they don't often send reporters to our games.

Time was, both newspapers in Indianapolis—the morning *Star* and the afternoon *News*—had beat writers assigned to the Indians that traveled to many of the road games. In the early days of my time with the Indians, Max Greenwald covered the team for the Star while Les Koelling covered for the News. Les also wrote a bowling column during the winter, so during those months he pronounced his name Ko'-ling. During the baseball season, he went with Kel'-ling.

After I became publicity director, I made it a point to alternate our press releases between mornings and afternoons so each paper would get its turn to be first with the significant stories. I was trying to be fair, but Bob Early, the managing editor of *Star*, always complained if his paper didn't get the break when a new manager was hired. He would call me on the phone and chew my fanny every time.

Regardless of the newspaper coverage, the Indians have always sought media attention to stay in front of our fan base. Given that, it might be difficult to believe I once nearly turned away ESPN from televising our game.

The Major League players were on strike in the 1981 season, so the teams sent their announcing crews to their minor league affiliates for the July 4 games around the country. We were playing Evansville, which was the Triple-A affiliate for Detroit. That meant we had legendary broadcasters Ernie Harwell and Paul Carey from the Tigers and Marty Brennaman and Joe Nuxhall from the Reds calling the game that night.

They joined our own Howard Kellman and Evansville announcer Larry Calton along with the announcers for the cable network ESPN, which was televising the game live from what was normally our organist's booth. With the strike benching all the Major League teams and with the Fourth of July holiday being such a popular day for baseball, ESPN wanted to air a minor league game.

ESPN was less than two years old at the time and barely known throughout the country. I had no knowledge of its existence, so when a representative called about broadcasting our game with Evansville, I told them they would have to pay their broadcast fee upfront. I believe it was about $3,000, a pittance today. But how was I to know if they would mail a check, or if it would clear?

They didn't pay in advance, but they did pay, and I was happy to have the exposure.

Unfortunately, the most widely covered game in franchise history didn't turn out well for us. We lost, 8 – 0, as Evansville's Larry Pashnick threw a five-hit shutout.

○

One of the things you learn from experience when you're a general manager is how to execute a postgame celebration after winning a championship.

A lot of cheap champagne gets sprayed around the locker room, so you have to protect your eyes. Beer flows, too, but the champagne really burns. It feels good because of the joy of the moment, but it's painful, too.

I also learned not to wear street clothes, so I wouldn't have to drive home soaking wet. I wore a bathing suit under my clothes during the game and then took off my pants and shirt for the celebration.

○

One of the most famous players ever to play for the Indianapolis Indians is Bob Uecker. Not because of his talent, but because of his legendary broadcasting career with the Milwaukee Brewers. He's a natural comedian and became nationally-known in the 1980s through television commercials and talk show appearances.

He played in six Major League seasons as a catcher from 1962 – 67. His lifetime batting average was .200, which gave him plenty of material for jokes, but he was an outstanding defender with a strong arm. His career with the Indians consisted of just eight games in 1960. We had him on loan from the Braves organization for the start of the season, but he was traded to Louisville in May.

He hit just .227 for us, but he had the highlight of an eighth-inning home run in a victory over Minneapolis less than 12 hours after his third child, a daughter, was born.

His popularity became obvious when we moved downtown to our new stadium in 1996. I thought it would be nice to put the name of a former star Indians player on every suite. I came up with 40 or 50 players, and then, as an afterthought, decided to throw Uecker's name into the mix. That suite name was in high demand, but Ray's Trash won out and still has it today.

Bob Uecker played in eight games for the Indianapolis Indians, batting .227 – but had one memorable hit.

○

I've never been a big drinker. Even while in college or the Army, I wasn't one to go out drinking with the guys. I just didn't have much of a taste for alcohol, and never wanted to be drunk or hungover.

One night, though, I lapsed.

After one of my early seasons as the Indians' general manager, Ownie Bush and I went to Chicago to meet with the officials from our Major League affiliate, the White Sox. We went to dinner at a fancy restaurant, one of those places with bathroom attendants. We had cocktails before dinner, and White Sox general manager Eddie Short kept ordering Canadian Club Manhattans. Trying to be courteous toward the boss, and probably feeling some peer pressure, I kept up with him.

I remember going to the men's room during dinner. After washing my hands, I took a towel from the attendant to dry them. I pulled a 50-cent piece out of my pocket to give him a tip, but dropped it on the floor because of my unstable condition. I bent over to pick it up, but he insisted.

I didn't sleep well that night and had a terrible hangover the next day. I resolved then I would never drink too much again, and I've kept that promise. Although I admit I've gotten a little tipsy after imbibing some champagne during championship celebrations in the clubhouse. That's a justified excuse!

○

One of our most memorable opening-day games was played in April of 2005, when 10,150 fans came to Victory Field to watch Curt Schilling pitch against the Indians.

What they wound up seeing was one of the highlights of Zach Duke's career.

Schilling was a six-time All-Star who had won 21 games and picked up a World Series victory for Boston's championship team the previous season. He had undergone surgery on his right ankle in the off-season and was on a rehab assignment for the Red Sox Triple-A affiliate, Pawtucket. His mere presence sold a lot of tickets for us. Even better, we won the game.

Schilling, 38 years old at the time, gave up seven earned runs in six innings in our 7 – 5 victory but received a standing ovation from our fans when he left the game. Duke, meanwhile, got the victory after allowing three runs and no walks in five innings. He was a 22-year-old prospect who had won a combined 15 games in Single A and Double A the previous season.

Schilling went on to go 8 – 8 for Boston that season, and pitched two more years after that. Even in his final season, at age 40, he had a 9 – 8 record.

Duke went 12 – 3 for us that season, then moved up to the Pirates. He went 8 – 2 as a rookie for them. He was still pitching in 2018 for his ninth Major League team, with a 66 – 90 career record.

He had a magical season in Indianapolis, however, and for more reasons than one. He met his future wife, Kristin Gross, while with us; she was our field emcee. They were married in Evansville in 2007.

○

Some of the scenes from the movie *Eight Men Out* were filmed at Bush Stadium in the fall of 1987.

I was offered a bit part in the movie about the Black Sox Scandal of 1919, but turned it down. I wanted to keep my focus on getting the park ready for our season after filming was completed. My son Bruce appeared briefly as a sportswriter, however.

We kept some of the changes the production company made to the park, and took advantage of their work in other ways, too. One day I was sitting in my office and saw a flatbed truck go by with our light towers on it. Baseball stadiums in 1919 didn't have lights, so they had to go. We took advantage of the opportunity and had them painted before they were reinstalled.

The producers invited the public to come out and fill the seats in our grandstand for some of the baseball scenes. They were given period clothing, and instructed when to cheer to provide a realistic setting for the game action in the movie. It was very cold during filming, and extras did not turn out in the numbers needed.

Ultimately, cardboard cutouts of fans were used to make the seats appear full. From a distance, you couldn't tell. I was amazed by the skill of the people making the movie to be able to do things like that.

○

From the time I became general manager in 1961, we were often in desperate need of revenue. We would have years where we were slightly profitable and then some where we lost money. Over my first 10 years or so, we pretty much broke even.

In the early 1970s, the worm began to turn. People began to enjoy minor league baseball for what it was. Throughout the 1950s and '60s, a lot of people complained about baseball being too slow, and the media discussed ways to speed up the game—ad nauseum, it seemed to me—but after the Vietnam War, it seemed people were more willing to relax and enjoy a baseball game.

Minor league baseball was perfect, especially during a recession, because ticket prices were reasonable. It also helped that there's less demand for winning in the minors. You always wanted to put a winning team on the field, but your control over the roster was limited and you knew you were destined to have some losing seasons. We wanted people to have an enjoyable experience even if the Indians lost, and didn't want the entire focus to be on the outcome.

Some minor league teams had "guaranteed win night," in which fans received a free ticket to a future game if the team didn't win. I never thought that was a good idea, because it shifted the emphasis away from family entertainment and made the games more serious than they needed to be.

Our move downtown in 1996 sealed our financial stability. We have 29 suites that go for $32,000 – $47,000 dollars per season, and most of them are sold on multi-year contracts. We also have some that are set aside for use on a per-game basis, and there's a strong market for those.

○

Temper tantrums are common in baseball. Most of them occur in private, away from the view of fans. We lost future Hall of Famer Randy Johnson for several weeks when he smacked a bat rack and broke a bone in his right hand. Usually, though, players don't inflict damage on themselves, only on inanimate objects.

A visiting player, for example, might take a bat and break all the light bulbs in the runway from the dugout to the locker room after striking out in a crucial situation or getting an umpire's call he thought was unfair.

Then I would have to call the general manager of his team and report the damages and tell him I would be sending him a bill. He would normally say he needed to call in the player and get his side of the story. The player might deny it at first, but eventually would fess up. The general manager then would ask for the bill, and more often than string you along and take his sweet time paying it, no matter how small.

Of course there were times I was on the other side of the situation after one of our guys broke something in another team's park. I would then sit down with the player and ask him about it. You owe him that much. The player would then have to write a check to the Indians to reimburse us for the check we sent to the other team.

Years ago we might have taken the amount out of a player's paycheck, but now checks are generated by the Major League team's office, so it's impractical to deduct a relatively modest amount to cover damages.

○

I often had to scramble to find a head groundskeeper for the Indians. Sometimes we'd be able to keep a guy for a couple of years, but other times we couldn't hold on to one for even that long.

One year in the 1970s, Ike Ives came to the rescue. He was retired from working for the Star, where he had been a printer. He joined us as a volunteer handyman, who performed duties such as painting, carpentry and plumbing. He knew I was having trouble with my search for a groundskeeper, so one day he volunteered himself for the job. Although he lacked experience in that area, I didn't have any better options, so I hired him.

We had a problem that season with the grass in shallow left field. It just wouldn't grow the way we wanted, and it never looked right. Ike didn't really have the expertise for that task, but he worked hard at it.

When it came time for our annual exhibition game against the Reds, we wanted the field to look good because we were going to have a full house. I had Ike get some green vegetable dye and spray the area so it would at least look good. Before the game, Cal Burleson said, "Ike's got that area looking pretty good out there!" I said, "It ought to be, we painted it green." Cal couldn't believe it.

I liked Ike, but he had a gruff personality and could be difficult to work with. Cal, when he was our business manager, couldn't seem to get him to do anything. Cal's desk was about 15 feet from mine, and one day he brought in Ike to give him instructions on a particular task.

He wasn't getting anywhere with Ike, and Cal finally became so exasperated he said, "I want you to know, I'm the business manager and you're the groundskeeper and you'll do what I tell you to do!"

You couldn't deal with Ike that way, though. He had been a valuable volunteer for us and was then working for a small salary. He had pride and understandably didn't like to be bossed around. I had gotten to know him well enough that he could confide in me, and he once told me he had spent several years in prison in the Chicago area.

I asked, "What the heck did you do to get in prison?" He just said he had gotten in with a bad crowd of guys.

○

Concession sales provide a major part of any professional sports team's revenue. I learned the hard way, however, to let someone else handle it.

At the end of the 1961 season, Indianapolis Motor Speedway president Tony Hulman recommended to our board chairman Frank McKinney Sr. that we operate the concession stands ourselves. The Speedway had done it, and it had worked well for them.

It was a good idea in theory. It cut out the middle man and could have left more profit for us. The problem was, I had no experience operating concessions. It's a unique business with many challenges and did not work for us.

We hired a man to check the game day reports for the concession stands, and he caught the manager changing the sheets and apparently pocketing some of the money, a total of several hundred dollars. I called the manager into my office and showed him the evidence. He asked for my forgiveness, so I told him if he would repay the missing money he could start over.

I looked him in the eye and said, "John, don't ever steal from the Indians again." He assured me he wouldn't.

But we caught him a second time, either later that season or the following season. I called him into my office again and showed him the evidence. I looked at him and held out my hand without saying a word. He reached into his pocket, handed over the keys and walked out the door. I never saw him again.

His wife called two or three weeks later and said, "I don't know what problem you had with John, but the one thing I can say to you is, John's an honest man."

I let her have her say, but didn't want to debate the issue.

Not everyone stole money from the concession stands, though. Some people stole food.

One night after a game I was walking toward the clubhouse in the concourse when I passed one of our concession workers, a heavyset woman, walking the opposite direction. Sticking out of her brassiere were six to eight raw wieners that I assumed she planned to take home.

I called our concessions manager and instructed him to tell her we no longer needed her services. I didn't want to make a big deal of it, but I couldn't let it go. If she was stealing wieners, she was capable of stealing other things, including money.

Issues such as those convinced me it was best to have companies that specialize in concession operations run them for us. They have expertise and volume buying power. We receive a percentage of sales under that arrangement, and we have a more professional concessions operation that results in an enhanced bottom line profit for the Indians.

○

The Indianapolis Indians once were mentioned in an episode of *I Love Lucy.*

The first episode of the sixth season of the classic sitcom, which aired in 1956, featured Bob Hope. He was one of the owners of the Cleveland Indians at the time, and Cleveland owned the Indianapolis Indians.

The premise of the episode was that Lucy was trying to get to Hope at a baseball game to convince him to perform at her husband Ricky's club. She dressed up as a vendor so she could approach Hope while he sat in the stands, but he was hit in the head by a foul ball while distracted by her attention.

Later, as he sat in the locker room receiving treatment, she walked in dressed as a player in order to get to him again.

"You must be that new rookie we brought up from our farm in Indianapolis," Hope said.

It's probably no coincidence that one of the show's head writers, Madelyn Pugh, was born and raised in Indianapolis.

○

Carl Erskine is one of baseball's greatest figures, and has been a friend of mine and the Indians for many years.

Erskine is a native of Anderson, less than an hour's drive north of Indianapolis. I saw him play a game in high school against Broad Ripple in Indianapolis, but could not have imagined the career he would have as a Major League pitcher. He played for the Brooklyn Dodgers from 1948 – 57, then moved with the team to Los Angeles and pitched in the 1957 and '58 seasons.

He threw two no-hitters for Brooklyn and was a 20-game winner in 1953. He struck out 14 batters in a World Series game in 1953, including Mickey Mantle four times, and was an All-Star in '54. His integrity was such that he retired at the age of 32 when he felt he could no longer perform at a high level, although Dodgers general manager Buzzie Bavasi encouraged him to keep playing.

He returned to Anderson upon retiring and became a banker. We were the nearest professional baseball franchise, so it was only natural he would attend our games occasionally. He did more than that, however, because he's the type of person who gets involved in his community.

He still comes to our games once a year as a fan. He brings friends from Anderson, sits in the stands and enjoys the game. On one occasion I was hosting the famous hockey announcer, Mike "Doc" Emerick, in a suite. Someone told me Carl was at the game, so I went down to invite him up to the suite to meet Doc. Carl and Doc began trading stories and the crowd inside the suite grew. People were even standing outside the door with an ear cocked, trying to listen.

Carl is an accomplished harmonica player, so we invited him to play at our Triple-A All-Star game that was televised on ESPN in 2001. He played "Take Me Out to the Ballgame" during the seventh-inning stretch. He told me later he received more calls for doing that on national television than for anything he accomplished as a member of the Dodgers.

Carl's an amazing person. He might not be deserving of selection to the Hall of Fame strictly on his playing career, but I believe there should be a place in Cooperstown for people such as him, who contribute so much to the game and to their communities.

His nickname "the Gentleman from Indiana," given to him by famed *New York Times* sportswriter Roscoe McGowan, says it all.

I answered the phone at my office on a winter Saturday to find Carl calling. He had forgotten to order a ticket for the Indianapolis Old-timers Dinner featuring his old Dodger friend Frank Howard.

"Was I too late to purchase a ticket?" he inquired.

I invited him to join the Indianapolis Indians' table that evening. A few bites into our salads, the emcee looked at our table and asked if Carl could till in for the absent invocator, which he did with aplomb. A student manager from one of Purdue University's athletic teams wowed the crowd with an impersonation of Howard Cosell as a preliminary dinner speaker. After a few sentences from Frank Howard that neither entertained nor informed, he sat down, and the dinner's organizers realized that they needed someone to save the program.

They once again called on Carl, this time to "tell some old Dodgers stories," which he did for about thirty minutes.

○

As the Indians' general manager, I wasn't my own boss. I had to answer to the board of directors, so my relationship with the chairman of the board was crucial—both to the team's success and my sanity.

Once the Indians became a publicly traded company, a board became mandatory. Frank McKinney Sr. was the first chairman. My relationship with him was good, despite my gaffe regarding the championship rings in 1961. He held the position from 1956 – 68, then gave way to Lou Hensley Jr., who was chairman until 1972.

That required an adjustment on my part. Lou was a fellow Shortridge graduate and a successful wealth manager and bond consultant for several Wall Street firms. He had a role in many of the important construction projects in Indianapolis, and was involved with many civic organizations.

He had limited knowledge of baseball, though. He was busy during the day, so he often called me at home at night and talked for as long as 30 or 40 minutes. That wasn't a call I enjoyed taking, because I already had put in a full day at the office. The fact he wasn't knowledgeable about the game made it that much more difficult.

He offered some strange ideas about promotions, too. He had a table at the Columbia Club, where he met with friends for lunch nearly every day. Occasionally he would invite me to join him and seven or eight other men to talk about the team. They sometimes would needle him about the team's attendance, which led him to tell me we needed better promotions. He would ask if we had tried this or that, and usually we already had.

One of his ideas, though, was truly original. He wanted to have our relief pitcher ride to the mound on horseback. When someone brought up the possibility of the horse relieving itself on the mound, he said that would be a great thing.

"I don't think it would be great, Lou," I said.

"Oh, it would get publicity all over the country," he said.

Fortunately, we never had to try that one.

I had a more stable relationship with Hank Warren Jr., who was our board chairman from 1978 – 86. My first meeting with him, however, was unforgettable.

Hank was the Vice-President of Marketing for Stokely Van Camp and had been influential in the development of Gatorade. I had been trying to get Stokely to sponsor one of our games without success, so I was referred to Hank. I went to meet with him over lunch at the University Club one day to seek sponsorship from Stokely.

He was angry, though, because a few days earlier, the federal government had ordered the company to recall Gatorade from shelves all over the world and destroy the bottles because of a concern over contamination.

Hank ranted about the recall throughout lunch. Finally, when we were ready to get up and leave, he said, "Max, what was it you wanted to talk about?" I gave him my pitch and he immediately said, "We'll take one."

He loved the Indians immediately, and eventually became chairman after a stint as a board member. He gave up his position in 1986 because the coverage under the Indians' liability insurance had been reduced and he and some board members believed they were at risk of becoming personally liable if a lawsuit were filed. I became the chairman until the issue was resolved, at which point Warren returned. I never had one argument with him in our years together.

○

(Left to right) Indianapolis Indians radio broadcaster Jim McIntyre, a Stokely Van Camp executive, and Max posed for a promotional photo for Stokely Van Camp night at Bush Stadium.

The inspiration for the ivy on the outfield walls at Wrigley Field in Chicago came from Indianapolis' original Victory Field.

Bill Veeck wrote in his book, *Veeck as in Wreck*, that Phil Wrigley had sent him on fact-finding missions throughout baseball in the late 1930s, and one of the places he went was Indianapolis. Veeck admired the vines on our outfield wall and suggested the idea to Mr. Wrigley, who owned the Cubs. Wrigley agreed, and vines were planted at Wrigley Field.

My best ivy story is the time we were playing Denver. We were batting in the bottom of the ninth with two outs and runners on base when one of our players hit a pop fly to short left field. Denver's shortstop backed up to make the catch, but dropped the ball and allowed our winning runs to score.

After the game ended, he was lying on the field. Most of the players had left for the clubhouse but a couple of Denver's players went over to console him. I was growing impatient because I wanted to shut off the outfield lights. They finally got him up but it took a while to get him off the field.

A few days later called few days later I called Denver's general manager, Jim Burris, to inquire how his player was dealing with the disappointment.

"He's OK now, but he has a helluva case of poison ivy," Burris said.

Apparently out of frustration, the player had walked to the outfield wall and yanked some of the ivy, and gotten into some poison ivy. It was unfortunate for him, but for us it was much better than grabbing a bat and slamming the water cooler or breaking light bulbs in the tunnel leading to the locker room.

○

Centerfielder Ken Berry, who played for the Indians in 1963 and '64, probably still stands as the greatest defensive outfielder in franchise history. He made the greatest catch I had ever seen to that point.

The chain-link fence that cut off a portion of the deepest part of center field had not yet been installed, so Berry had to patrol an area that extended 480 feet from home plate to farthest point of the wall. And on Sept. 8, 1964, in a late-season game against Oklahoma City, he covered nearly all of it.

With Rusty Staub on first base, Jimmy Wynn—who later became famous as The Toy Cannon for the Houston Astros—hit a ball deep to centerfield near the flagpole that stood 470 feet from home plate. Berry got a good jump on the ball and sprinted toward the wall, then turned

Ken Berry, shown with manager Les Moss, earned team MVP honors for the Indians in 1964.

his head just in time to make the catch while in a dead sprint. It was an instinctive play, one very few outfielders in any era could make.

Berry downplayed it, telling newspaper reporters it was "the luckiest catch I ever made."

He added: "I didn't know it was that dark out there. I lost the ball, turned where I thought it would be, and it fell into my glove."

Nobody who saw it considered it lucky, though.

"I've never seen any better," our manager Les Moss said.

Berry, whose nickname was The Bandit, had been a wide receiver on Wichita State's football team and gave credit to that experience for his fielding ability. He was voted our Most Valuable Player that season, and then was called up to the White Sox for the rest of the season. He went on to play into the 1975 season for the White Sox, Angels, Milwaukee, and Cleveland.

The sad thing about his catch was that only 835 fans were in attendance that night. But I'll bet most of them remembered it for the rest of their lives, as I have.

○

Outfielder Dave Schneck had played three seasons for the Mets before joining us for the 1975 and '76 seasons. He hit just .250 and .251 those years, but provided a few memorable moments—including one courtesy of my wife Judy.

Schneck added to our July 3rd fireworks display at Bush Stadium in '76 when we played a doubleheader against Evansville. He hit a solo home run in the first inning, then drove a game-winning three-run homer over the right field wall in the bottom of the seventh, the final inning of the first game. He came back to hit another home run in the second game to help the Indians to a 2 – 0 victory. He finished with five hits in seven plate appearances that night, and drove in five of our six runs.

Later that season, several of our front office staff members and a few Schumachers, including Judy, gathered in the Perry Room after another home game. The conversation reflected everyone's frustration with the sub-par performance of several players and the team's disappointing record.

Suddenly, Judy mounted a chair to make her point more effectively: "Dave Schneck has given me more thrills and excitement than anyone this season!"

To say the least, that rare but memorable display of exuberance by the mother of four, not to mention the unintended entendre, got everyone's attention.

Judy was supportive of Max's career throughout the ups and downs.

○

Former Oakland Athletics owner Charlie Finley was famous for being difficult. He built teams that won the World Series in 1972, '73, and '74, but his irascible nature made plenty of enemies along the way.

I got a taste of it in 1968, when our affiliate in Cincinnati was to play the A's at Bush Stadium on Sunday afternoon, April 7, in the final exhibition game before the regular season began. Civil rights activist Dr. Martin Luther King Jr. had been assassinated three days earlier in Memphis, Tennessee, and rioting had occurred in some major cities throughout the country as a result. Indianapolis had been spared, however, because Robert Kennedy, who was in the city while campaigning for President, gave a calming impromptu speech.

Finley called the Indians office the day before the exhibition game to say he was under pressure from the American League office to cancel the game. I was flying back from Spring Training in Florida at the time, so Finley talked with our business manager, Terry Stewart. Terry told him that Indianapolis had avoided rioting and the game could be played, but Finley wasn't convinced. Terry finally told Finley he would have me call him when I returned.

I called Finley and told him the same thing Terry had said: the game could be played. Finley kept insisting it be cancelled, however. The Reds and A's had played exhibitions in Birmingham, Alabama and Shreveport, Louisiana the two previous days with no problems, but Finley kept saying he was under pressure not to play the game and would not bring in his team. Sunday had been declared a national day of mourning for Dr. King and some other exhibition games had already been cancelled.

I called Reds general manager Bob Howsam, and we agreed we had no choice but to cancel the game. As Howsam said, we couldn't play a game with just one team. We each notified our local media outlets to inform the public and make it official.

Finley later called back and said he wanted his team to use our stadium for a practice on Sunday. It already was committed to flying to Indianapolis, so he wanted it to use the opportunity to prepare for the start of the regular season.

I tried to be diplomatic.

"Mr. Finley, since we're not able to play the game, I've decided to give our staff the day off."

"Don't worry about that," he said. "We don't need the staff to be there. We'll let ourselves in and then just leave when we're done."

"Mr. Finley, we don't do things that way around here," I said.

He persisted. Finally, I ran out of patience.

"Mr. Finley, the ballpark will be locked tomorrow," I said, and hung up the telephone.

The cancellation was a blow to the Indians and our fans. The Reds and A's both would barely manage a winning record that season, but they were forming the nucleus of their championship teams of the 1970s. Pete Rose and Johnny Bench were playing for the Reds, while Reggie Jackson, Bert Campaneris, Catfish Hunter, Rollie Fingers, and Blue Moon Odom were among the members of the A's.

We offered fans holding tickets to the game the right to exchange them for any of our regular season games that season. But there was no way to recover the money we had spent on advertising and promotion for the game, and we were not going to receive our share of the income generated by the game.

The A's flew to Indianapolis on Saturday as scheduled and stayed overnight, but flew to Baltimore Sunday morning. They opened their season there on Wednesday when the season opened after a two-day delay.

○

One of the great things about baseball is the endless variety of possibilities with every pitch. Each game offers fans the opportunity to see something they've never seen before, even someone like me who's seen thousands of baseball games.

Two such instances occurred in recent years at our downtown Victory Field.

In 2012, when the Indians were playing an evening playoff game, an opposing player hit a line drive down the left field line. In midflight, however, the lights went off and the field was smothered in darkness. It turned out an automobile had crashed into a nearby electrical transformer.

Indianapolis Power and Light made prompt repairs and play resumed before long. I don't recall the umpire's ruling on the matter, and whether or not the batter was awarded a base or went back to the plate, but it was something I never had seen before.

Another memorable game occurred in 2018, when two Indians hit for "the cycle" by collecting a single, double, triple, and home run in a 12 – 5 victory over Lehigh Valley. Catcher Jacob Stallings and shortstop Kevin Newman each accomplished the rare feat in the eighth inning with a triple and home run, respectively.

Obviously, the odds of that happening are incredibly small. But that's baseball. Go to enough games, and the odds are that eventually something crazy will happen. ⬢

AFTERWORD BY RAZOR SHINES

When I think about Max Schumacher, it gives me a feeling I can't really explain. I love the man dearly. ● I have no doubt that he's the number one reason my career took off after I joined the Indians at the age of 27 and was still playing for them when I retired at 36. I also never would have had the opportunity to become a major-league coach or a minor-league manager. He was always in my corner, and I owe my career to him, really.

I played for seven minor-league teams and one major-league team over 16 seasons, but Indianapolis has always felt like home to me. One time when I was with the Montreal Expos but not playing much, Max called them and said, "Look, if you're not going to play him, we can sure use him here." When the Expos told me around one p.m. they were going to send me down, I asked them if I could leave immediately. I really wanted to play that night, and I did. Max was the main reason for my devotion to the team and the city.

Max was way ahead of his time. He should have been a major-league general manager. This man knew baseball, he knew how to bring people to the ballpark and he knew what winning was about. He also maintained a high standard of integrity for all of his employees, players included. But he stood up for his players when he believed they weren't being treated fairly by the major-league team. Believe me, that's not how it works with all baseball franchises.

I batted .282 and drove in 80 runs my first season with the Indians in 1984. I was then called up to Montreal and batted .300 for the Expos over 12 games, but injured my knee in a base-running accident the final day of the season. I had surgery that winter and worked in a meat packing plant in Wichita, Kansas to make ends meet. The Expos thought I was holding out, but I was just trying to get back into shape before playing again.

I reported to Max on July 4 and he gave me another chance, probably against the wishes of Montreal's front office. A lot of minor-league general managers wouldn't have done that, and it allowed me to revive my playing career.

Max also tried to help me when I had an offer to join Pittsburgh in spring training and take a shot at making their roster in 1990, rather than rejoining the Indians. He warned me of the risk I was taking and told me the Pirates probably weren't being honest with me about my odds of making their team. But when I decided to take the chance, he sent me off with his blessing and no hard feelings. He just wanted what was best for me.

He turned out to be right, of course. After a season playing for the Pirates' minor-league affiliates in Mexico City and Buffalo, I returned to Indianapolis and played the last three seasons of my career there.

Here's another example of Max's loyalty to his players. I once joined the Muncie Symphony Orchestra to read the poem "Casey at the Bat" at one of their concerts. Max and his wife, Judy, drove an hour to attend it. Players don't forget that kind of thing.

It was a great pleasure for me to play for Max and an even greater pleasure to know him. You knew you would be treated fairly and be part of an organization dedicated to winning. Just understand that after all these years, if there's anything lowly Razor Shines can do for Max Schumacher, it's a done deal.

—Razor Shines

ACKNOWLEDGMENTS

I would like to thank Howard Kellman for his encyclopedic memory which helped fill in some gaps, Cheyne Reiter for pulling together many of the photos that appear here, and Bruce Schumacher for fact-checking and editing.

BIOGRAPHIES

Max Schumacher worked for the Indianapolis Indians for 60 years as the ticket manager, publicity director, general manager, president, and chairman of the board. He led the way in establishing the organization as a model Triple-A franchise that has achieved sustained excellence and profitability and remains the envy of professional sports teams throughout the country.

He has frequently been recognized for his contributions to baseball and the city of Indianapolis. He was named a Sagamore of the Wabash, a state honor, in 1980. He received the John H. Johnson Presidents Award as the minor league baseball figure who "exemplifies the standards of a complete baseball franchise" in 1988, and was recognized as the King of Baseball for lifetime service to the minor leagues in 1997.

The Indians have accordingly been honored during his association with the franchise. *Baseball America* declared them the Triple-A Team of the Decade for the Nineties and they received the Bob Freitas Award for excellence in Triple-A baseball in 1996 and 2014.

He also spearheaded the effort to build a downtown ballpark, Victory Field, which opened in 1996. It has been recognized as the best minor league stadium in America by both *Baseball America* and *Sports Illustrated*.

Schumacher was the captain of the baseball team at Shortridge High School, from where he graduated in 1950. He also was a member of the baseball team at Butler University, from where he graduated in 1954 with a Journalism degree. He was inducted into Butler's Athletic Hall of Fame in 2005.

He remains involved with the Indianapolis Indians as the Chairman Emeritus.

Mark Montieth has been widely honored for his work as a sportswriter and radio host in Indiana. A 1977 graduate of Indiana University, he is the author of two previous critically acclaimed books. "Passion Play: A Season with the Purdue Boilermakers and Coach Gene Keady" was published in 1988, and "Reborn: The Pacers and the Return of Pro Basketball to Indianapolis" was released in 2017. He was inducted into the Pike High School Hall of Fame in 2015 and the Indiana Sportswriters and Sportscasters Hall of Fame in 2018.